HOPE FOR THE CHURCH OF ENGLAND?

HOPE FOR THE CHURCH OF ENGLAND?

Edited by

Gavin Reid

KINGSWAY PUBLICATIONS

EASTBOURNE

ISBN 0 86065 457 7

Front cover photo: Andy Williams Photographic Library

Printed in Great Britain for
KINGSWAY PUBLICATIONS LTD
Lottbridge Drove, Eastbourne, E. Sussex BN23 6NT by
Richard Clay (The Chaucer Press) Ltd, Bungay, Suffolk.
Typeset by CST, Eastbourne, E. Sussex.

Contents

INTRODUCTION

THE CRISIS FACING ENGLAND'S CHURCH

by

*Gavin Reid**

'Crisis' is an overworked word, beloved by early editions of evening newspapers. It is used so often and in so many contexts that the suspicion of 'crying wolf' is firmly built into all our reactions.

Nevertheless I can think of no other word appropriate to the Church of England at the moment. The crisis it faces is a convergence of several unrelated problems, all of which have 'gone critical' at the same time.

The first element in the mix is *the crisis of chronic decline*. As with most mainline denominations numbers have been declining at least since the first World War. In the twenty-five years since my ordination I have seen the number of confirmations virtually halved, the numbers coming forward for ordination suffer a similar fate, and average Sunday church attendance drop to about 3% of the national population.

All this would be a serious matter for any denomination, but it is particularly serious in what is the established church of the realm with its Bishops in the House of Lords and its General Synod being described (by the Queen, no less) as 'a

*Gavin Reid is Secretary for Evangelism with the Church Pastoral Aid Society and was seconded for three years to be National Director of the Mission England project from 1982 to 1985. He is the author of several books and is a Director of Kingsway Publications. He is a member of General Synod and serves on the Board for Mission and Unity. Married to Mary, a teacher, who became editor of *Family Magazine* in 1984, he has three grown-up children.

forum for the expression of Christian opinions on the quality of our national life'. The Church of England, viewed in numerical terms, is a minority group within a minority group. What is more, it is a minority group that is still shrinking in numbers to the tune of 1% per annum.

Such chronic decline has a basic effect on morale. I sense that underlying almost every official report and developed strategy coming from the Church of England, there is a resignation to the inevitability of decline. At best, we tend to strategize out of a constructive pessimism.

As numbers decline, giving is affected. We face enlarging demands with diminishing resources. As congregations have a developing sense of being 'quaint' and increasingly out-of-step with surrounding society, there is the growing temptation to turn away from the challenge of such odds, and seek solace in a Christianity of small concerns and personal preferences.

The second element in the mix of problems is *the crisis of doctrinal uncertainty*. This is, perhaps, endemic in the Church of England, but it came dramatically to a head in the controversy over Professor David Jenkins' appointment to the senior Bishopric of Durham in 1984. This crisis has been well stated in David Holloway's book *The Church of England—where is it going?*

What came to light with the so-called 'Durham affair' did not start with it. As later contributions in this book will show, the history of the Church of England and its very rootedness in the moderation-loving English temperament lies behind what has happened and what is always likely to happen. The Church of England is an accommodating church, eager to embrace all who live in its parishes; and yet it seeks to be a credal community calling upon its ministers to assent to doctrinal positions and to work under authority.

In practice what has happened is that the Church of England prides itself in being '*comprehensive*'. It holds together a coalition of traditions and individuals with differing ways of expressing Christ-related religiousness. There is the charitable assumption that everyone within its grasp is loyal to the creeds which are recited at every service. The secret of unity rests on two unwritten laws. First, that nobody blows the gaff on his or her unorthodoxy too publicly; second, that nobody else will persecute or prosecute for heresy.

What David Jenkins did in 1984 was to break the first of those laws, and what people like David Holloway have done is break the second. The general public and the many in the pews who were hitherto blissfully ignorant are now aware that a doctrinal crisis exists and that something must be done. As I write these words, the bishops are reluctantly having to talk together about the limits of comprehensiveness and to make a statement of their common belief. This is something very different from a church doctrinal commission producing a report that can be received as 'useful for discussion'. This is 'for real'! The Bishops are defining an official position.

The bluff has been called, and it is hard to see a result that will keep the Church intact.

In the meantime, the public revelation of the Church's inability to define its beliefs and to discipline its members has played into the hands of other Christian groupings and denominations which have no such inhibitions. Since the crisis came to a head in 1984, we have seen a slow trickle of people leaving for the Roman Catholic and Orthodox Churches on the one hand, and a stronger flow heading towards the house churches on the other.

Which leads us naturally to the third element in the mix— *the crisis caused by the attractiveness of new, exciting Christian congregations*. For some twenty years the 'charismatic renewal' has been affecting the long-established churches of our country (and, indeed, many other countries). It has claimed to have been inspired directly by the Holy Spirit of God (which makes dialogue with its adherents difficult!) and it has sought to open up personal experience and public worship to the reality of the living God. Several of the contributors to this book would claim—as I do—to have benefited in various ways from this movement.

As the renewal movement progressed, it became clear that two things were happening. Some committed to the renewal were conscientiously sticking to their existing affiliations.

Others were either feeling rejected or were concluding that the existing churches were beyond renewal. A new start in terms of congregational life was needed. There had to be a *restoration* of the New Testament Church with its apostles and prophets; its disciplined and interdependent congregations; its freedom in worship and its conviction that God acts supernaturally in everyday life.

The 'house churches' began. Meeting initially in homes, they mushroomed and coalesced into lively, self-confident congregations hiring halls and buying old church buildings to cope with a growth rate estimated in 1985 to stand at 29% per annum.

To join with such a fellowship in worship is to experience liveliness, youthfulness, a contemporary feel to the music (which is often led by electronic instruments), and a general feeling of certainty about where everyone is going.

Of course, this type of congregational experience is not every believer's cup of tea. Some write it off as shallow, excitable and escapist. Colin Buchanan's criticisms in this book are more theological. However it is not hard to see how attractive these fellowships, and this exuberance and simplicity in worship, can be to very many people—especially young adults—who find the liturgical worship and 'fuddy-duddyness' of much Church of England activity to be joyless and irrelevant to life.

It is only too understandable that the house church members have high morale and cannot avoid proselytizing—especially in schools and colleges. The remarkable growth of these new fellowships has been nearly always at the expense of other more traditional congregations. They are only beginning to make their own converts to any significant degree. Tom Walker in his contribution to this book reveals something of the difficulties and fears that a Church of England vicar can feel as he sees people drawn away into these new, beguiling congregations.

The fourth element in the mix is *the crisis in the understanding of ministry*. For centuries it was plain sailing. The church was served by an elite clerical caste—bishops, priests and deacons. There were two unchallenged assumptions. First, this was self-evidently the way to order things. Second, ministry was a male preserve. The various schools of thought within the church (such as Anglo-Catholics and Evangelicals) have, at times, differed sharply and fiercely, but there has always been total agreement about these two assumptions.

This is no longer the case. The decline in numbers coming forward for ordination and the rise of an increasing number of self-evidently gifted lay men and women has forced the church to think more flexibly about lay ministry and non-stipendiary, part-time clergy. The charismatic movement has raised again the whole New Testament concept of varied gifts and ministries shared by all in the congregation. The tight threefold order of ministry—bishops, priests and deacons—simply doesn't square with need, experience or Scripture. A ferment over ministry is taking place in which many of the developments are positive, but there is a negative side. Many clergy feel undermined and devalued. Many are scratching around trying to find a new role. Others are fighting rearguard actions.

And what about the place of women in all this? Here the situation becomes explosive. In the outside world a battle for women's rights is taking place. Male stronghold after male stronghold is falling before the sheer logic and justice of so much that feminists are urging. Laws are being changed to accommodate many of their demands. What then should the church do with regard to ordination? Is it the last bastion of sexism in excluding women from the priesthood—or are there important theological issues at stake? Is the heartfelt cry of many women for ordination simply a reflection of trends in the surrounding secular society, or is it based on a sense of calling from God and the discovery of long overlooked scriptural understandings?

Whatever the answers may be, few things more divide the Church of England at the present time than the issue of the ordination of women.

The final element in the mix is *the crisis in Church/State relationships*. The Church of England enjoys a privileged position as the established church of the nation. The Queen is both head of State and head of the Church. Bishops are nominated by the Prime Minister and have to receive royal approval.

Sir Timothy Hoare, in his contribution on establishment, makes a strong plea for the church to see and exploit the missionary potential of the arrangement, but as congregations diminish and as governments take on an increasingly secular flavour the Church/State relationship becomes more and more anomalous.

Against this background there is a political dimension. Should the government of the day be entitled to expect support (or at least silence) from the Church to which it grants such privileges?

In recent years there have been a considerable number of public clashes between Members of Parliament (usually of a Conservative complexion) and clergy who have been adjudged to have 'meddled in politics'. 'Leave politics to the politicians,' comes the cry, 'and stick to talking about God!'

When the Archbishop's Commission on Urban Priority Areas was published in December 1985 there was a near-hysterical reaction from some backbenchers, and something less than fair comment from senior government figures. The report was thinly disguised left-wing collectivist thinking, we were told. One M.P. called for church-going Tory voters to reduce the amount they put in the collection plate as a protest.

The problem is that behind the posturing there was an element of truth on both sides. The perceptions of some parliamentarians were not totally incorrect. At a time when the Church seemed reluctant to make clear pronouncements on doctrine, it was strange that some of its bishops and clergy could show such dogmatism in matters relating to the social and political realm. At the same time—as Pete Broadbent shows in his contribution on 'the Political Imperative'—it is impossible to bear witness to a righteous God who loves all of his creation, yet stay silent or inactive when one sees sections of the community getting a raw deal. To stay silent at such times is to bear false witness. This is the dilemma that the Christian faces. If one is to obey the commandment to love one's neighbour, then some sort of 'politics' is inevitable.

In the summer of 1985 an apparently innocent piece of ecclesiastical legislation came before a thinly attended House of Commons. It had been sent from the General Synod to get its expected parliamentary 'nod'. The measure dealt with the abolition of a 'largely meaningless Tudor formality in the election of bishops'. It failed to get the necessary approval. In the thinly attended session it was an easy task for a group of M.P.s to score a symbolic victory against a Church they were beginning to despise. As a reaction to 'unbelieving Bishops' and a Church 'meddling in politics', they made their point.

Little harm was done, but a clear signal was sent out that parliament and government could flex a few muscles if it so intended, and it should not be forgotten that the Prime Minister still has a real element of choice with regard to the appointment of bishops.

This book is called *Hope for the Church of England*. It is written against the background of this multiple crisis, at a time when other Christian groupings are growing dramatically while the Church of England's figures continue to decline (albeit in less alarming proportions to those of previous years).

My strategy as editor has been simple. I have gone to a number of intensely committed Anglicans, all of whom share my own stance within the Evangelical tradition. This ensures a certain consistency of approach among us, but the book is not presented as a party 'line' or a manifesto. We do not all agree among ourselves at every point.

There is a certain significance at this moment in drawing all my writers from the Evangelical camp. The recent *Faith in the City* report has placed on record the fact that 'irrespective of location, churches where the clergy classified themselves as "evangelical" have higher Sunday attendances . . . than those which describe themselves as "high church" or "middle of the road".' In terms of apparent numerical success (a very relative term, however) Evangelicals have perhaps some right to make a few points.

My authors were asked to write about their commitment to Christ through the Church of England, and against the background of the crisis facing the Church. They have tackled their task in different ways. Some reflect; some report; some criticize; none are bland.

The Church of England is, at the end of the day, the people within its ranks. My writers are typical of thousands in pulpit and pew whose commitment is first and foremost to Christ but who see the Church of England, for all its weaknesses, as the right way through which to serve their country as well as their Lord.

PART ONE

The Church

I

I BELIEVE IN THE CHURCH OF ENGLAND

by

*John R. W. Stott**

Let me begin by spelling out my priorities. First and foremost, by God's sheer mercy, I am a Christian seeking to follow Jesus Christ. Next, I am an evangelical Christian because of my conviction that evangelical principles (especially *sola scriptura* and *sola gratia*) are integral to authentic Christianity, and that to be an evangelical Christian is to be a New Testament Christian, and vice versa. Thirdly, I am an Anglican evangelical Christian, since the Church of England is the particular historical tradition or denomination to which I belong. But I am not an Anglican first, since denominationalism is hard to defend. It seems to me correct to call oneself an Anglican evangelical (in which evangelical is the noun and Anglican the descriptive adjective) rather than an evangelical Anglican (in which Anglican is the noun and evangelical the adjective).

Attitudes to the Church of England have varied greatly from generation to generation. People have oscillated somewhat unsteadily in their views from euphoria to despair. For example, in the eighteenth century William Grimshaw,

---

*Dr John Stott became Rector Emeritus of London's famous All Souls' Church, Langham Place after twenty-five years of distinguished service as Rector. He travels extensively throughout the 'Third World' where he has a particular concern to encourage and equip emerging church leaders. He has been a central figure in the dramatic resurgence of evangelicalism in the Church of England since the Second World War. He was Director, and is now President, of the London Institute for Contemporary Christianity. He has written many books and is a Chaplain to the Queen. Birdwatching is his favourite relaxation.

writing to his friend John Wesley, said: 'I believe the Church of England to be the soundest, purest and most apostolical Christian Church in the world. Therefore I can with good conscience (as I am determined, God willing, to do) live and die in her.'

In the following century, Thomas Arnold expressed the opposite extreme. He wrote in 1832: 'The Church, as it now stands, no human power can save. . . . When I think of the Church I could sit down and pine and die.'

In our own twentieth century Archbishop Robert Runcie, when he introduced and opened the Partners in Mission Consultation in 1981, confessed that the Church of England 'arouses both fury and enthusiasm'. He recalled how on one occasion in the House of Commons, when the Church of England was coming under criticism, a member shouted out, 'Hands off the Church of England; it's the only thing that stands between us and Christianity!'

As for myself, I believe in the Church of England. At least, I do and I don't. I do not believe in the Church of England, of course, in the sense that I believe in God—Father, Son and Holy Spirit—as the object of my confidence and worship. Yet I do believe in the Church of England in the sense that I am deeply grateful to be a member and a minister of it, and to be able to remain such with a good conscience. So before I come to the difficulties, I will sketch four distinctive features of the Church of England, which also constitute four reasons why I belong to it.

First, the Church of England is *a historical church*. It is, in fact, the church of the English people. It traces its origins back not to Henry VIII and his matrimonial problems (the notorious 'King's Matter'), but to the first century A.D. when the Roman legions were colonizing the empire, and merchants followed them, and among these soldiers and tradesmen there must have been followers of Jesus Christ. Both Tertullian and Origen round about the year 200 A.D. spoke of a church in England. St Alban died as a martyr for Christ probably during the Decian persecution of 250 A.D. At the Synod of Arles in 314 A.D. there were three British bishops. So the Church of England is the historic church of this country.

Now this historical dimension is important today in a world that is busy cutting adrift from its historical roots. For the living God of the Bible is the God of history, the God of Abraham, Isaac and Jacob, the God of Moses and the prophets, the God of our Lord Jesus Christ and his apostles, and the God of the post-apostolic church. One of the weaknesses of the house-church movement is that it has little sense of history, little sense of continuity with the past.

Secondly, the Church of England is *a confessional church*. We move now from history to theology. According to 1 Timothy 3:15, the church is 'the pillar [*stulos*] and bulwark [*hedraiōma*] of the truth'. *Hedraiōma* may mean either 'bulwark' or 'foundation'. In either case it holds a building firm, while pillars thrust the building aloft. So the church is called to serve the truth, both holding it firm and holding it high for people to see. The Church of England, therefore, has doctrinal standards and a confession of faith. The Book of Common Prayer and the Thirty-Nine Articles remain the doctrinal basis of the Church of England, in spite of the weakening of the formula of assent and the arrival of the Alternative Service Book. Moreover, these standards affirm the supremacy of Scripture over traditions, the sufficiency of Scripture for salvation, and the justification of sinners by grace alone, in Christ alone, through faith alone. These three doctrines are particularly dear to evangelical believers, and they are plainly affirmed in our Anglican Articles.

It is true that there are a few church leaders who deny some fundamentals of the faith, and this is both a tragedy and a scandal. But the Church of England has never abandoned its confession of faith. It is a confessional church.

Thirdly, the Church of England is *a national church*. It is not a 'state' church like the continental Lutheran churches, but it is an 'established' church (recognized by law and given certain privileges), and—more important—it is a 'national' church because it has a national mission. In ideal and purpose, then, the Church of England is neither a sect, nor a denomination, but the church of the nation, with a responsibility to be the nation's conscience, to serve the nation, and to bring Christ to the nation.

It is perfectly true that in practice this ideal often breaks down, and that at the end of the twentieth century adjustments are needed. For instance, the parochial system needs to be overhauled, as the Tiller Report suggests. Nevertheless, although adaptations are necessary, the Church of England remains a national church.

Fourthly, the Church of England is *a liturgical church*. It has a Book of Common Prayer, and an Alternative Service Book, containing services for public worship. Some say that set services inhibit spontaneity and the freedom of the Spirit. This does not have to be the case. Form and freedom are not necessarily incompatible with one another. Certainly, we welcome the greater flexibility which the ASB has given us. But rightly it has not abandoned a liturgical framework and form.

Why should we value a liturgy? First, there is plenty of biblical warrant for liturgical forms. The New Testament contains many snatches of ancient hymns and credal statements, for Christians took this over from the Old Testament. Secondly, a liturgy enshrines truth and safeguards uniformity of doctrine. Thirdly, it gives a sense of solidarity both with the past and with the rest of the church in the present. Fourthly, it protects the congregation from the worst idiosyncrasies of the clergy. Lastly, it is an aid to concentration and to congregational participation. These are great gains. They make me thankful that the Church of England is a liturgical church.

Here then are four reasons why I believe in the Church of England. It is the historical church of the English. It has a sound biblical, theological basis. It is entrusted with a national mission. And it has in its liturgy a worthy vehicle for the praise of almighty God through Jesus Christ in the power of the Holy Spirit.

At the same time, having made these positive statements, many evangelicals feel uncomfortable in the Church of

England today. The Church of England which I have described is more of an ideal than a reality. Some would dismiss it as a 'paper' church, and not one of flesh and blood, bones and sinews.

So in the last few years there has been what some have called an 'Anglican evangelical identity crisis'. I never liked the expression myself; I think it was alarmist and inaccurate. Yet many have had an identity problem, and have felt a certain malaise, even a disorientation. It is mainly due to the period of rapid change through which we have been passing, and to the difficulty we all have in adapting to change. It is not easy to maintain our own identity when other identities are changing all around us. Our evangelical movement has been growing in size, stature, maturity, scholarship and cohesion.

At the first National Evangelical Anglican Congress at Keele in 1967, we made a public, penitent renunciation of the 'piety' which had spoiled so much of our witness hitherto. We had previously had our backs to the wall, and suffered from a siege mentality. At Keele, however, we emerged from our ghettos. We strongly affirmed our continuing evangelical convictions. But we also declared our intention to share responsibly both in the visible church and in the secular world.

Ten years later at the second National Evangelical Anglican Congress at Nottingham, which was twice as large as Keele, we became aware of the diversity of the evangelical movement. We realized that it contains different strands (e.g. reformed and charismatic), and had become more a coalition than a party. At the same time, there has been an assault (especially since the 1960s) on traditional Christian doctrine and morality, mounted by so called 'secular' or 'radical' theologians. It has been disturbing that some of our leaders have been influenced by it. In consequence, the loyalty of ordinary church people has been strained.

So what should we do? I would like to outline the three options that are before us, the two different kinds of 'comprehensiveness', and the five things we ought to be doing.

Three options

The question is this: how should evangelical churchmen react when the majority of Church of England members are not fully evangelical?

The first option is *separation* or *secession* from the church. 'To stay in a doctrinally mixed church,' some are saying, 'is an intolerable compromise. It gives the impression that we condone heresy. So, in order to maintain our evangelical testimony without compromise, we must get out.'

This is the position of independent evangelicals. Their overriding concern is to preserve the doctrinal purity of the church, which indeed is a right and proper concern. We should share their zeal for the truth, and their courage. But they tend to pursue the purity of the church at the expense of its unity, for which they seem to have no comparable concern. To be sure, there could be an extreme situation (e.g. if the church were officially to repudiate the incarnation), when the only possible course would be to secede, since then the church would have ceased to be the church. We need to remember, however, that the sixteenth-century Reformers were themselves very reluctant schismatics. They did not want to leave the Catholic Church. On the contrary, they dreamed of a reformed Catholicism, a Catholic Church reformed according to Scripture, and were concerned for both its purity and its unity. Calvin wrote to Cranmer in 1552, for example, that the separation of churches was 'among the greatest misfortunes of our century'. The 'bleeding' state of the body of Christ affected him so deeply, he added, that he would 'not hesitate to cross ten seas' if he could help. 'Indeed, if learned men were to seek a solid and carefully devised agreement according to the rule of Scripture . . . I think that for my part I ought not to spare any trouble or dangers.' That is (or should be) exactly the position of Anglican evangelicals today.

The second option that is before us is the opposite extreme. It is that of *compromise,* and even *conformity.* This is the decision of some who say not only that they intend to stay in the Church of England at all costs, but that they would be willing to lose their distinctive evangelical witness. Some younger evangelicals are saying that they no longer wish to be labelled 'evangelical'. They just want to be 'Christians'. Some seem to mean by this that they see no point in maintaining distinctive evangelical doctrines or distinctive evangelical structures (like Diocesan Evangelical Fellowships).

I respect their desire to be responsible members of the Church of England, and (when it can be done with integrity) to minimize the differences between the traditions in the Church of England. But I think that their position is short-sighted. For we should have the courage, with humility, to bear witness to evangelical truth as we have been given to understand it. We claim no infallibility, and may be mistaken on certain points. We are open to have our minds changed if Scripture can be shown to require it. But we cannot conceal or smother our convictions. Our concern as evangelicals should certainly not be loyalty to a 'party'. Talk of a 'party' is a political concept. It conjures up toeing the party line, sub-mitting to the party whip, and accepting the party discipline. Evangelical loyalty is not to a party, however, but to revealed truth, and in particular to the unique glory and adequacy of Jesus Christ.

The essence of the evangelical faith is that in Jesus Christ incarnate, crucified and exalted, God has spoken and acted decisively and finally for the salvation of the world. In consequence Jesus Christ is God's last word to the world, and it is inconceivable that there should be any higher revelation than what he has given in his Son. Jesus Christ is also God's last deed for the salvation of the world, and it is inconceivable that anything should need to be added to it. Nothing can be added either to what God has spoken in Christ or to what God has done in Christ. Both were *hapax,* 'once and for all'. In Christ God's revelation and redemption are finished and complete.

Of course, we have a great deal more to learn, but God has no more to reveal than he has revealed in Christ in whom the fullness of the Godhead dwelt bodily. Again, we have a great deal more to receive, 'grace upon grace upon grace', but God has no more to give than he has given in his incarnate Son who died and rose again. In fact, the supreme ministry of the Holy Spirit is to enable the church to understand ever more fully what God has revealed in Christ and to receive ever more fully what God has given in Christ. To attempt to add anything to Jesus Christ, either to add words of our own to his word, or to add works of our own to his work, would be dreadfully derogatory to the perfection of his person and his work.

That is why the hallmark of evangelicalism is an insistence on *sola scriptura* and *sola gratia*. They arise from *solus Christus,* Christ alone for revelation and redemption. Our concern, then, in maintaining a distinctive identity is not to be awkward or unco-operative or cussed or partisan. It is to be faithful to the unique glory of the person and work of our Lord Jesus Christ. It is, we believe, for the good of the church and for the glory of God in Christ, that we should maintain our distinctive evangelical witness.

The third option is *comprehensiveness without compromise,* that is, staying in without caving in. Frankly, it is the most painful of the three options. It causes one considerable 'misery', which is the word that Dr Jim Packer has used in his excellent Latimer monograph *A Kind of Noah's Ark.* The other two options are easier because they are ways of cutting the Gordian knot. The first is to separate from everybody you disagree with, and so enjoy fellowship only with like-minded Christians. The second is to decline to maintain a distinctive testimony, and so regard all viewpoints as equally legitimate. These are opposite options (separation and compromise). But they have this in common: they are both ways of easing tension and escaping conflict. You either get out or you give in. The harder way, which involves walking a tightrope, is to stay in, while at the same time refusing to give in. This means living in a permanent state of tension, declining either to compromise or to secede.

Let me sum up. The way of separation is to pursue truth at the expense of unity. The way of compromise is to pursue unity at the expense of truth. The way of comprehension is to pursue truth and unity simultaneously, that is, to pursue the kind of unity commended by Christ and his apostles, namely unity in truth. Thus, Jesus prayed in John 17 for the truth, holiness, mission and unity of the church, while in Ephesians 4 Paul affirmed that there is 'one Lord, one faith, one baptism'. Unity and truth always walk hand in hand in the New Testament.

Two kinds of comprehensiveness

I have described the third option as 'comprehension'. I now have to qualify this. For what is often called the 'comprehensiveness' of the Church of England can be sought in one or other of two ways. On the one hand, there is an unlimited and unprincipled kind of comprehensiveness, from which no one is excluded. On the other hand, there is a limited and principled kind of comprehensiveness which lays down clear lines of demarcation.

I begin with the unlimited and unprincipled kind. This is the modern notion of what has been termed the 'glorious' comprehensiveness of the Church of England. It is a doctrinal free-for-all, in which no opinion is prohibited, let alone condemned as heretical. Rather, every viewpoint is welcomed as a contribution to, and even ingredient of, the resulting pot-pourri. It is this that Bishop J. C. Ryle dubbed 'a kind of Noah's ark', roomy enough to accommodate both the clean and the unclean.

The best lampoon of this view was developed by Ronald Knox in the marvellous piece which he entitled 'Reunion all Round' and included in his *Essays in Satire*. It was sub-titled 'A plea for the inclusion within the Church of England of all Mohometans, Jews, Buddhists, Brahmins, Papists and Atheists'. In the new and universal church which he saw emerging, 'nobody will be expected to recite the whole Creed', he wrote, 'but only such clauses as he finds relish in; it being anticipated that, with good fortune, a large congregation will usually manage in this way to recite the whole

Formula between them.' Having dealt with differences between Christians, and differences between Theists, he came finally to 'the Problem of Reunion with the Atheists'. In their case: 'We have only one single Quarrel to patch up, namely, as to whether God exists or not.' So he proposed to the Theologians that, as we believe God to be both Immanent and yet Transcendent, we should be able to reconcile ourselves to 'the last final Antinomy, that God is both Existent and Non-existent'. He ended: 'Thank God, in these days of Enlightenment and Establishment, everyone has a right to his own Opinions, and chiefly to the Opinion, That nobody else has a right to theirs. . . .'

This is not true ecumenism, however, but syncretism. Jesus our Lord and his apostles warned the church of false teachers. And I am glad that the Church of England has always officially recognized that unity must be in truth and that comprehensiveness must be principled.

Take, for example, the report *Church Relations in England*, published in 1950 soon after Archbishop Geoffrey Fisher had preached his famous Cambridge University sermon about the Free Churches 'taking episcopacy into their system'. That report, by representatives of the Church of England and the Free Church Federal Council, said that 'assurances with respect to doctrinal standards having been mutually exchanged, each church would declare itself satisfied that the other maintained the apostolic faith and proclaimed the apostolic gospel'.

Eleven years later at New Delhi, when the Third Assembly of the World Council of Churches produced its important definition of 'the unity we seek', it described 'all in each place who are baptized into Jesus Christ and confess him as Lord and Saviour' as being brought by the Holy Spirit 'into one fully committed fellowship, holding the one apostolic faith, preaching the one Gospel' and 'breaking the one bread'.

Ecumenical endeavours do not always seem in practice to fulfil this ideal, but at least in principle the goal has been well expressed, and Anglican evangelicals are committed to it. For instance, when in 1978 more than a hundred Anglican evangelical leaders addressed an Open Letter to all the Archbishops and Bishops of the Anglican Communion on the subject of Anglican relations with Catholic and Orthodox churches, we made the unambiguous statement that the only possible basis for union would be 'tested theological agreement'.

Moreover, we must not imagine that we are the only people in the church who care about revealed truth. In spite of our dissatisfaction with some elements of the Final Report of the first Anglican Roman Catholic International Commission, it clearly says that 'there are essential matters where it (sc. the Commission) considers that doctrine admits no divergence'. In other words, there are certain central truths which cannot in any circumstances be surrendered. Anglicans should be embarrassed that it is Roman Catholics who seem to be insisting on this more strongly than they. Thus Cardinal Hume has gone on record as saying: 'I am uneasy concerning the comprehensiveness of the Anglican Church. Comprehensiveness has been seen by the Anglican Church as a matter of pride. I wonder,' he went on, 'whether it is not its Achilles' heel—leaving the rest of us asking: what does the Anglican Church, as a church, hold to be essential?'

So now let me move on from the unlimited and unprincipled kind of comprehensiveness, which we should firmly reject, to the limited and principled kind, which is the historic understanding of what true Anglican comprehensiveness is all about. The purpose of the Elizabethan settlement in the sixteenth century was to unite the nation within a national church committed to the supremacy of Scripture and to the catholic creeds. As Roger Beckwith has written, 'the Articles are the *confessional* expression of this faith, and the Prayer Book the *liturgical*'. It was a policy, in Dr J. I. Packer's words, which 'expressed doctrinal modesty, but not doctrinal indifferentism'.

In 1957 Dr Alec Vidler had referred to the two kinds of comprehensiveness which we are discussing. In his *Essays in Liberality* he wrote:

In these latter days the conception of Anglican comprehensiveness has been taken to mean that it is the glory of the Church of England to hold together in juxtaposition as many varieties of Christian faith and practice as are willing to agree to differ, so that the Church is regarded as a sort of league of religions. I have nothing to say for such an unprincipled syncretism . . . . The principle of comprehension is that a church ought to hold the fundamentals of the faith, and at the same time allow for differences of opinion and of interpretation in secondary matters, especially rites and ceremonies . . . .

It is essential to distinguish between these two visions of comprehensiveness. For one is a virtue, the other a vice. That is the language of Dr Packer, who in his contribution to the symposium *Evangelicals Today* (1973) distinguished in these terms between the two ideals. One is 'the *virtue* of tolerating different views on secondary issues on the basis of clear agreement on essentials' (which was the stance of the Reformers), while the other is 'the *vice* of retreating from the light of Scripture into an intellectual murk where no outlines are clear, all cats are grey, and syncretism is the prescribed task'. It is a distinction which goes right back to the apostle Paul's insistence on loyalty to the apostolic faith, alongside liberty of conscience on secondary issues.

An agenda for Anglican evangelicals

So far I have mentioned historical, theological, national and liturgical reasons for belonging to the Church of England, and for remaining a member of it with a good conscience, provided always that our church continues to distinguish between true and false, principled and unprincipled, forms of comprehensiveness, and abides by the distinction faithfully.

What, then, should evangelicals be doing in the Church of England? Have we an agenda for action? Let me make a few suggestions.

First, we should *maintain our evangelical witness*. The best and most positive contribution which evangelicals can make in the prevailing climate of doubt and dispute is to remain courteously but firmly evangelical, that is, to bear witness to the biblical faith. To sweep our differences under the carpet, and pretend that we all believe the same thing really, would be a horrid hypocrisy. It is much more conducive to the health of the church to maintain our convictions with integrity. Preachers need to take more trouble to expound and apply Scripture from the pulpit, and parents to teach it to their children at home. We should also be praying that God will raise up more evangelical scholars, who will devote their lives to 'the defence and confirmation of the gospel', that is, to a reasoned evangelical apologetic.

Secondly, we should *develop theological dialogue*. I am aware that in some circles the word 'dialogue' sets red lights flashing, for it is branded as being necessarily an essay in compromise. In itself it is nothing of the kind, however— although it may be used in the service of compromise. Instead, it is an indispensable expression of Christian courage, humility and integrity. For a dialogue is quite simply a responsible conversation in which each side is willing to listen as well as speak, to learn as well as teach. In such a situation it takes courage to bear witness, humility to listen openly, carefully and respectfully, and integrity to be willing to adjust either one's own position or one's perception of the other person's, if either has been shown to be skewed.

Over the past decade or two I have myself been involved in dialogue with several different groups, not of non-Christians but of professing Christians of various persuasions. I can say without hesitation that each has been profitable. For when we keep our distance from one another, and our only contact is to write books and articles against one another, grotesque caricatures develop in our imagination, until we can distinctly see in the other's profile the shape of horns, hooves and a tail. But when we meet face to face (or 'eyeball to eyeball', as our American friends like to say), we discover that the other person is indubitably a human being, not a demon, and usually a reasonable one as well. Then, as we listen to each other, we find common convictions and concerns. And when, in areas where we differ, we listen more attentively still to the real issues which the other wants to safeguard, we at least understand, and sometimes even find that we want to safeguard them too.

CEEC (the Church of England Evangelical Council) has encouraged the formation of a number of different dialogue groups (e.g. with Roman Catholics, Anglican Catholics, independent evangelicals, Free Church evangelicals and charismatics), and I feel sure will continue to do so.

Thirdly, we should *remember the apostolic strategy*. The apostle Paul refers in most of his letters to false teachers who in one way or another were disturbing Christ's church. He gives various instructions on how to deal with them. But his long-distance strategy is often overlooked. One of the reasons why he left Titus in Crete, he wrote, was to 'appoint elders in every town', whose qualifications included a firm hold on 'the trustworthy message as it has been taught', so that they would be able both to 'encourage others by sound doctrine' and to 'refute those who oppose it'. Why was this necessary? Because 'there are many rebellious people, mere talkers and deceivers', and 'they must be silenced' on account of their ruinous influence (Tit 1:5–11, NIV). In other words, when false teachers increased, Paul's strategy was to multiply the number of true teachers. I myself believe that, when church historians come to trace and evaluate the post-war resurgence of the evangelical movement in the Church of England, they will recognize the strategic influence of the six evangelical theological colleges.

Fourthly, we should *press for ecclesiastical discipline*. To be sure, I hope that controversy will always remain distasteful to us, and heresy-hunting even more so. Nevertheless, there is still a place for doctrinal and moral discipline in the church. In principle, as we have seen, the purity of the church (in both faith and life) is a desirable goal, even though we recognize that its complete purity will be attained only at the consummation.

Probably most evangelicals would still subscribe to the booklet commissioned by CEEC in response to *The Myth of God Incarnate* (1977) and entitled *Truth, Error and*

Discipline in the Church (1978). In it we made it clear that we had no wish to inhibit theological exploration (e.g. into the mystery of the Incarnation) or genuine intellectual enquiry (for questions have to be asked, not stifled) or academic freedom. At the same time, if a clergyman is no longer able conscientiously to teach one of the central truths of the historic faith, which he has solemnly undertaken at his ordination to teach, then his only honourable course is to resign. What if he declines to do so? The booklet hedged its answer with proper safeguards. Its conclusion was that if a fundamental Christian doctrine is at stake, and if the ordained minister concerned is not questioning it but denying it, and if he is not passing through a temporary period of uncertainty but has reached a settled conviction, and if he refuses to resign, then his bishop should take appropriate legal steps to withdraw his licence or permission to teach.

Fifthly, we should *preserve our personal consistency*. Our responsibility before God is not only to defend and proclaim the evangelical faith verbally, but also to 'adorn it', that is, 'make it attractive' (cf. Tit 2:10), by our consistent Christlike behaviour. Our evangelical forebears were more committed to the pursuit of holiness than we are. We may now regard their vision as too pietistic, and we may not agree with all their holiness teaching, but we cannot fault their 'hunger and thirst for righteousness'. It is an indispensable characteristic of all authentic evangelicalism. So we need more evangelical holiness, which exhibits the power of the gospel to transform sinners into the image of Christ, and more evangelical churches which exhibit the power of the gospel to make our worship real, our fellowship caring and our outreach compassionate. Without doubt the best way to commend 'the faith of the gospel' (the evangelical faith), both individually and corporately, is to live a life that is 'worthy' of it (cf. Phil 1:27).

So I do believe in the Church of England, in the rightness of belonging to it and of maintaining a faithful evangelical witness within it and to it. For I believe in the power of God's word and Spirit to reform and renew the church. I also believe in the patience of God. Max Warren wrote in his

I Believe in the Great Commission that 'the history of the Church is the story of the patience of God'. He was right. I do not think we have any liberty to be less patient than God has been.

Note: This chapter has been adapted from an address given to the Guildford Diocesan Evangelical Fellowship in November 1984.

2

WHY I BELONG TO THE CHURCH OF ENGLAND

by

*Peter Hall**

The simplest answer to the question, why do I belong to the Church of England, is: by accident! I happened to be born in England, I was sent to the Church of England as a child. Having left home and left any kind of church attendance behind, I happened to be attracted to hear someone preach the gospel in a Church of England church. Having accepted Christ, and discovered that I now needed to go to church again and belong to a community of Christians, it seemed most natural to go back to the Church of England that I already knew. My new-found faith was, among other things, the out-working of my baptism as a baby and confirmation in early teens. At that stage I did not seriously question taking my place in the church where those things had been ministered to me. Within a fairly short time, investigating the possibility of being ordained as a minister of the church, the Church of England once more seemed the obvious place in which to test out that calling.

None of that is particularly 'spiritual'. 'Why the Church of England?' did not seem to me, probably because of my temperament, to be a terribly important question. I think that

---

*Peter Hall, Bishop of Woolwich, served for ten years as minister of a suburban church in Zimbabwe (then Rhodesia) before returning to be vicar of the church where he was once curate—St Martin's-in-the-Bullring, Birmingham. He is chairman of the Evangelical Urban Training Project and has a particular concern to see the cultural divides of class and race crossed with the gospel.

had circumstances accidently pushed me in the direction of any of the mainstream Protestant denominations instead, it would have caused me little anxiety, and I would have equally cheerfully explored the possibility of belonging, and being ordained in such groups. One of my earliest experiences after becoming a Christian was to worship in a small Baptist chapel in Northern Spain, with stones rattling on the window because of the hostility of the local, predominantly Roman Catholic population. I remember being very comfortable with the 'Baptistness' of that congregation—it was its 'Spanishness' that was strange to me.

I know now, however, that I belong to the Church of England for glad and positive reasons. I have become much more consciously aware that it is the right out-working for me of my Christian experience and pilgrimage. I will try to select the things that have come to matter most to me.

A parochial church

I began theological study, with the possibility of ordination very quickly after accepting Christ as my Saviour. I did not really take part in the ordinary life of a parish again, because I was a student and was travelling a good deal, until I arrived as a new deacon in the centre of Birmingham. What has been very important to me ever since is the 'given-ness' of the parish, surrounding the actual building which is a Church of England church. In the small villages and old-established small towns, the parish church was visibly the centre of the community, physically, socially and spiritually. That model, which dies very hard in the mind and imaginations of many people, does not, of course, hold in our huge urban industrial areas; but with every church, nevertheless, there is a parish—a geographical area in which people live, work, and in which many things are present which are part and parcel of the material of human life.

The building is still very public (though sadly today often closed outside service times) and so anyone can come to it who thinks there might be a way of satisfying whatever his or her needs are. The group of people who worship in it cannot protect themselves from the demands of the world around, without a very considerable defensive effort (which, of course, many such groups make very successfully!). But the parish remains there almost as a threat, unless its relationship with the worshipping congregation is embraced, welcomed, and obediently responded to, as God's call to the concerns of his kingdom.

As an ordained minister in such a church, I have never been allowed to forget the world around, nor to ignore the great sea of folk religion and religious experience in so many people's lives. I have never been free to turn away from the immensity of human need, on all levels, nor to evade the pressure to share my faith with so many who do not understand it, experience it, or necessarily want it.

Of course, we all have to face something in our own nature which will desire to worship piously, meet with other Christians, *and yet evade the responsibilities that the place and the community press upon us*. Any group of members of the Church of England can negate all these things, can build a little private club of people who worship in the church and use it for their own needs, can successfully freeze out by their own style of life anyone from the parish who might be different, yet wants to be involved. But the parish remains.

I detect today in a number of people, whose Christian belonging is expressed in the more private atmosphere of house churches, a real desire to relate to the rest of the community in the way that the parish system encourages.

In terms of how we understand our faith, the parish presents issues to do with the kingdom of God to the congregation that meets within its boundaries. When there are houses and flats in the parish that are obviously unfit to live in, and people who are completely homeless, our own sense of what is fair and just is challenged. Our distress about it drives us back to our Lord, who reveals himself concerned passionately about the justice that is not being done. Places of work in the parish, whether office or factory, raise equally sharply issues to do with the quality of people's lives. At whose expense is that quality gained—especially if the factory produces very bad smells or poisoned fumes, or the offices demand so many workers that the parish is carved up by the enormous demands of commuter transport to get them in and out? Our distress about these things brings us back to a Lord who is both calling us to share in his creative work, and concerned utterly that our working lives should be characterized by love, fairness and justice.

The parish, then, keeps always in front of our vision the fact that the kingdom of God, and his concern for human life, is something far bigger than the church, and than the religious dimension of our lives. I thank God for the parish system.

A national church

The Church of England is very obviously '*English*'. That may seem hardly worth saying, but I believe it has important theological consequences. We rejoice today whenever the work of missionaries over the last two hundred years (many of whom were from Europe) has resulted in a truly indigenous church. It is a sign that the gospel is taking root in any country when the Christian community begins to express its new-found faith in forms of worship and life which are truly belonging to that culture. We worry whenever the church goes on being simply a copy of what it is somewhere else. The Church of England expresses in its buildings, worship, and in its formulation of the Christian faith, things which are very deep in the English temperament. That is not to say that other Christian denominations have not been moulded by being English—they all have. But the national church has been interwoven with the life of the nation in a more complete and thoroughgoing way.

I became acutely aware of this on leaving England and going to work in the Anglican Church in what is now Zimbabwe. The task was to discover Christ as perceived through the eyes of the African Christians, through their worship and style, and to begin to disentangle what in myself was to do with being a Christian, and what was to do with being

English. It made me realize how well fitted the Church of England is to address English people, though not (to my frustration at that time) those of Zimbabwe. On the negative side, I also saw how very 'tribal' the Church of England is, and how difficult it is for anyone not of that tribe to penetrate it, and be accepted at every level. This is one of the reasons for rejoicing in the recent appointment of the first black bishop in the Church of England. He is a person who in his own right is clearly called to that kind of responsibility and leadership in the church, wherever he might be, but his presence proclaims now that the Church of England is part of Christ's whole church—however truly and rightly it expresses the Christian faith as it has been embraced by English people.

What are these English characteristics which I value? One of them is certainly a spirit of moderation, and a suspicion of anything that might look like fanaticism. I heard an American Christian (who was not an Anglican) praying on one occasion in thanksgiving for—'the Anglican Church—moderate in all her ways'. His experience, of course, was of American Anglicans, but it is a characteristic which the Church of England has given to the world-wide family of Anglican churches which has sprung from it. Another characteristic is a certain practicality and impatience with ideology. We are as a nation concerned with whether things will work, much more than whether they are of a pure ideology, whether they are rational, or whether they truly plumb the depths of human passions. Of course, Englishness can be quite disastrous—the counsels of moderation and the counsels of practicality would have prevented Christ from ever choosing the way of the cross. All I am saying is that these two qualities are very deeply rooted in the English temperament, and they therefore come out in our faith because the Church of England is a profoundly indigenous organism.

The theological consequence of these two qualities in which I do rejoice, and which I believe has been to the health of the church, is *a refusal to over-define*. The doctrines of the Church of England, beginning with the definitions of the *Thirty-nine Articles* (which sprang out of the particular controversies of the Reformation) are notably reticent. Definition is only ventured upon when the controversies force it, and large areas of belief and practice are left to be expressed in forms of worship, in the services of ordination, and to the conscience of individual Christians.

A refusal to define inevitably creates tensions. The Church of England today is once again struggling with the problem of 'drawing the line', beyond which it is not proper for a person to be either a leader in the church, or regarded as a faithful member of it. I believe this to be a far better tension, and a far more worthwhile struggle, than the constant efforts to reach doctrinal purity by over-definition. The latter has created as much division in the Protestant churches as it has amongst those seeking ideological purity in left-wing politics.

A church free from idolatries

You may be thinking that the matters which make me rejoice in the Church of England are not the directly theological issues which ought to decide a person's membership of any denomination. I would want to contest that view, because I believe the question of the indigenous nature of the Church of England to be a highly theological issue, arising from the doctrine of the incarnation. I also believe the question of the parish system to be profoundly theological, arising from our response to Jesus' proclamation of the kingdom of God.

However, I turn to the matter of *authority in faith*, which is one that everyone accepts as 'theological'. I rejoice in the restrained statement of Article 6 of the *Thirty-nine Articles,* which gives final authority to Holy Scripture. Scripture is given a supreme place, yet the title word 'sufficiency', and the words 'contains all things necessary to salvation' avoid any suggestion of idolatry of the written word. They allow for flexibility in the relationship between every written word in the Bible and God's word speaking to us, yet the whole of the Scriptures are held together as that which has authority. We are not led by the wording of the Article into unnecessary battles over every single word, nor over every apparent discrepancy between one part of Scripture and another.

I rejoice also in the clear statement of the authority of the tradition of the church as expressed in the three creeds, and in the on-going authority of the church to 'decree rites or ceremonies and have authority in controversies of faith'. The church is clearly stated 'to be witness and keeper of Holy Writ', and yet at the same time is said to be in error from time to time. Thus there is no idolatry of the church either. Furthermore judgements have to be made by individuals because the church might be in error. Thus human reason is also given authority, but it also is liable to error—'the condition of man . . . is such that, he cannot turn and prepare himself, by his own natural strength and good works, to faith and call of God'. There is therefore nothing in the Articles that can lead us to an idolatry of reason.

Such an understanding of authority, vested in the Old and New Testaments, interpreted by the traditions of the church, and by the exercise of human reason, is one in which I rejoice. It seems to me to defend us from exactly those idolatries which we are commanded 'to flee' by the New Testament, whether they be hidden under the respectabilities of idolatry of the Bible or of the church. Perhaps in our particular generation we need, more than either of those, *to be protected from the idolatry of human reason*, which in the last two centuries has dismissed so much human experience which reason alone, whatever its considerable achievements, could not encompass. I rejoice in an understanding of authority which finds its source in God himself, because it has resisted the alluring corporate temptation to make an idol either of the means whereby he communicates with us, or of the forms which he has given us to express the body of Christ in the world.

Another question I ought to face is: what would make me leave the Church of England? I would have to go back over the three things I have already said in order to answer that question, as well as include two more. I would leave the Church of England if it abandoned the parochial system. By this, I do not simply mean the closing of churches because of lack of clergy, or inability to cope with old buildings (both harsh realities to be faced). I mean if it departed from a sense of being involved in the wider community (now 'the parish') and retired into 'religion', in the narrow sense of the life and doings and the worship of the church community. Jesus called us to share in the building of God's kingdom, and not just in the building of the church.

An Archbishop's commission on the poor areas of our cities is therefore a faithful response to this calling, and its accurate grassroots reflection of what is really happening would be far more difficult to achieve without the parish system which exists in all such areas. Can the Church of England in general react to its revelations with equal faithfulness?

I would also leave the Church of England if its 'tribal' nature were so powerful a strait-jacket that it lost track of being part of the world-wide Christian church, and, for that matter, of the world-wide Anglican Communion. There is a real danger in our age of the Church of England lagging far behind even its own daughter churches in understanding God's purposes in the world today, and being imprisoned in the narrow tribalism that made people of Nazareth reject Jesus so violently when he spoke to them in the Synagogue (Lk 4).

I would leave the Church of England if it were to abandon its understanding of Holy Scripture as having final authority in matters of faith, and allowed either tradition or human reason to be 'equal' with it. We have already seen in Christian history that when either the tradition of the church or human reason is held to be equal with Scripture, it means in fact to be superior, and any sense of obedience to the Scriptures which are sufficient for salvation is lost.

Two other quite separate matters would concern me to the point of wanting to leave the Church of England: I have not mentioned precisely the doctrine of justification by faith, although it has been deeply embedded in much that I have said. I would leave the Church of England if any suggestion were allowed to creep into its formularies which made the source of our justification anything other than by receiving the grace of God through faith in Christ. I say particularly its *formularies*, because in practice I believe we do seek justification in other ways. An onlooker without knowledge of Christian faith would today judge us to be a whole body of people who are seeking justification by morality, decent living, and general respectability of life. It is just because this is so that I am urgently concerned with what is stated in our Article 11: *we are justified by what Christ has done for us through faith, and somehow we have to begin again to bear witness to that.* How can the nation of which we are members begin to see that we are justified in that way and in no other?

On quite a different track, as a member of an established church, I would leave if the full-time servants of the church were paid directly by means of national taxes. This is the case in the Lutheran family of churches, and I believe it to be disastrous in its spiritual effects. The Church of England is learning slowly and painfully, as the resources on which it has lived from the past grow less through inflation, to live by the faithful stewardship and giving Christians of this generation who are its members. That is a vital and health-giving process which must be hurried on as quickly as possible. Were any attempt to be made to divert that process, by using a taxation method (which, incidentally, would include non-Anglicans), we its employees would become in a very real sense servants of the state. I would certainly be unable to continue as one of its paid employees, or indeed one of its members.

All that is negative, and admittedly it is not an exhaustive list. What it really means, of course, is that I rejoice in the positives. I rejoice in the positive of the doctrine of justification by faith, because I believe it to be the very heart of what Christ came to do for us; and I rejoice in the struggle to enable us, together as members of the Church of England, to abandon all other forms of justification. I am glad to be a member of a church in which the understanding of authority helps me to flee idolatry; whose very Englishness helps me to witness to my own people, and to share in the process of incarnating Christ in our generation, provided I am not a paid servant of the State. And I am glad to be in a church where the ever-present parish keeps before us the vision of God's kingdom, challenges us to be obedient to his call of justice and compassion, and fills us with a painful longing for the coming of the new heavens and new earth.

3

ON LOVING THE CHURCH OF ENGLAND

by

*Colin Buchanan**

I was till recently the principal of a large Anglican Theological College. This was a marvellous place in which to get a glimpse of the future—for many of the future leaders of the Church of England were each year going through the institution. And I detect that many fine men and women of the gospel will be giving direction and character to the Church of England in the years beyond 2000—when I shall be safely in retirement or glory. So I would be a happy Anglican for those forward-looking reasons, if for no others. I am also aware that many of these ordinands were not brought up in the Church of England, but have by deliberate decision moved over to it. Far from being a sinking ship, the Church of England is undergoing renovation (or 'renewal', if one prefers less latinized words), and she is daily taking on board new gifted craftsmen who will assist the process.

Of course, there are always those on the other side who leave the Church of England—and some of them do take the view that she is a sinking ship on which they can do no good. And there are those on the ship who are unconvinced about

---

*Colin Buchanan, Bishop of Aston since 1985, has spent most of his ministry in theological education at St John's, Nottingham, where he became princi-pal in 1979. He founded the remarkable Grove Booklet publishing operation which publishes on a wide range of theological and pastoral subjects. He has been one of the outstanding figures in General Synod and played a signifi-cant part in shaping the Alternative Service Book. His special interests are liturgy and ecclesiology.

the future. So I write to discourage the leavers and to encourage the uncertain stayers. And I am fairly clear that in the last analysis the issue is not so much one of snuffing the wind as of getting doctrinal priorities right.

Choosing a church

Most of what I have written above damages my own position! I have been writing on the presupposition that there is ample choice for today's English Christians as to where they can 'belong'.

Even in the strongest evangelical or charismatic circles there seems to be a sense that 'belonging' to a church is correct discipleship—but the question of *which* church or fellowship that involves is seen as one for individual decision or choice. As a matter of observed fact, probably few such Christians make their decision on strictly doctrinal grounds, but they are influenced rather by proximity to a given building (though this matters less in the age of the motor-car), or by being taken by friends, or by enjoying the preaching, or the worship, or the ethos, or the warmth, of a particular congregation.

The churches themselves have generally come to terms with this multiplicity of choice, and they all attempt charitably to recognize each other as perfectly valid groupings. This approach flows with the milk of Christian kindness, but it does make the *raison d'etre* of any particular congregation or connection harder to distinguish. Often it seems that worshippers are saying that this grouping *does* exist (and has perhaps existed for two hundred years or more) and therefore it *must* exist, *must* take its share in the offering of a good choice to believers, and *must* (obviously) constantly work to build itself up. Yet its distinctive rationale remains impossible to discern.

Not so, however, with newborn assemblies. They usually have a much stronger self-confidence or sense of distinctive calling. In the last decade and a half we have seen this particularly with the rise of the so-called house churches. They tend to denounce 'denominationalism', and to call believers out of the historic churches into their fervent and loving groups. While they might allow that individuals must come to their own conclusions at their own speed, yet the basis of gathering is that the visible churches have declined until they are not recognizable as the people of God. They believe that individuals ought to leave and join in 'restoring the kingdom'. In the event, of course, these groups simply add to the denominational scene—it is only those with the most concentrated tunnel-vision who can sustain the notion that they have transcended denominationalism. So the choice which I set out in the paragraph above may now have widened to embrace both those groupings which basically affirm the Christianity of others, and also those groupings which basically deny if not the Christianity, at least the adequacy of others. *But it still presents itself as a choice.*

Various exclusive kinds of groupings have been with us for centuries in any case—whether in the original Anabaptists, or the Brethren Movement of the nineteenth century, or the exclusivism of movements such as Campus Crusade, or the new house church or restorationist phenomenon. So the difference is *not* as to whether a choice is set before believers, but as to how the different bodies view the other ecclesiastical options which are open to individuals.

But it is the principle of choice which worries me! We cannot of course change the hard facts of the English ecclesiastical landscape simply by not liking it, or by wishing it to be otherwise. But we can determine in our minds whether (as with sin, or perhaps with a chronic illness) we have to live with it, in tension with it, and to go on looking for a more truly healthy and biblical pattern in the future. This is part of our proper 'eschatological tension'—the sense of living uncomfortably with the present in order to work for the reform of the present pattern over the future. Any kind of teamwork teaches Christians this same tension—whether the teamwork of an eldership or the teamwork of a marriage relationship. In each case strains and frictions should make us work the harder for reform and improvement—it is sad indeed when they lead to opting out for the sake of self-preservation, or, even worse, self-indulgence.

It is also sad when defects in relationships become treated as norms of teamwork, and people resolve the 'eschatological tension' in favour of the defective present! It is my contention that this is what has been happening with denominationalism and the consequent 'choice' of places of worship. We ought, rather, to see it as *defective,* and yet live with it. The flanking alternatives, to which my teamwork illustration above pointed, are that we should either abhor the defect in such a way that we 'opt out of denominationalism', or that we should so come to terms with denominationalism that we treat it as a good not an evil. To many today, the opting out is the attractive option, but (as with marriage, etc.) those who opt out in fact take their problems with them—and 'opting out of denominationalism' in fact creates yet further congregations, more choice, increasing divisiveness, and thus (at least from where the angels sit) greater confusion.

I shall come on to the New Testament, but I conclude this section by noting that no one would wish this situation onto Third World Christians. Thus, in the nineteenth century, even the missionary societies which did not really trust each other, could nevertheless agree that, if there are over half a million Indian villages, it would be pointless for ten societies each to send a hundred pioneers to the same hundred villages. Even the most doctrinally hard-edged, or denominationally unyielding, could see that not only would nine hundred villages lack the gospel, which might by better strategy receive it, but also the effect on the actual hundred evangelized villages might be appalling! So they agreed a principle of 'comity', which might today look like an imperialistic carve-up, but was actually intended to secure 'areas of influence' which would maximize the thrust of each society, and preserve the villages from the perils of 'sheep-stealing' or of cut-throat competition in running loving communities!

Thus, to this day, in many parts of India there is one Christian community or congregation, and it is this single grouping which constitutes *the* Christian church in that village. It is not necessarily so in towns in India, of course.

But surely, almost even before we consider the New Testament, this pattern of there being *the* Christian church in each place, visibly and recognizably the point of 'belonging' of the disciples of the Lord Jesus—that is something each of us would covet.

The church in the New Testament

So now we come to ask these questions of the New Testament. It is clear that in the beginning, following the Day of Pentecost, all the disciples were together, sharing their meals, supporting each other with their worldly goods, and displaying a unity before the world. The effect of this was that to be converted a newcomer had to be converted *into the fellowship, into the community*. There was no gospel for the individual which first of all converted him, then asked him to choose to join a Christian fellowship. To belong to the Lord at all, he had to belong to the Lord's community. Baptism is not exactly our subject here, but in fact baptism was all of a piece with this kind of conversion. Today we consider conversion, baptism, and joining a church, as three separate steps in a disciple's pilgrimage—to the apostolic church they were all the same step, and came simultaneously. The convert was incorporated into Christ by the Spirit—by conversion, in baptism, into the Christian community. So the gospel was embodied in a single local community, and the call to conversion, to repentance and faith, was a call for inclusion in that community. Without that, the local church could not have recognized the new 'convert' *as* a convert.

This is the background to the insistence on the unity of the church in 1 Corinthians. In chapter 1 Paul writes that the Christians must not, even cannot, divide into separated groups. Their witness to their Lord is bound up with their own oneness—their fellowship witnesses to Jesus as their Lord just because it is one and is loving. To divide over matters of style or taste or preference or personalities would be to witness to either a divided Christ, or a lordship of someone other than Christ. I have not set out the specific verses here by way of commentary, but anyone who doubts the point has only to read the chapter with these questions in mind and will come to these conclusions. There is no scope in 1 Corinthians for groups of less than all the Corinthian Christians to gather on a voluntary basis and treat themselves as a local congregation or unit of the universal church.

This point is amply reinforced in chapters 11 to 13. In chapter 11 the local fellowship is being disrupted by unlove— unlove shown by the well-heeled to the poor. Astonishingly, from Paul's point of view, this unlove is demonstrated at, of all places, the Lord's Supper. Participants who show unlove to those who have gathered with them in fact fail to 'discern the Lord's body'. In other words, they have not understood that the Supper is to bind into a single unity those who eat and drink at it. Some words of the previous chapter reinforce this strongly: 'We, who are many, are one body, for we all partake of the one loaf.' Thus to establish two 'communions' would be to suggest, if not actually to create, two bodies. But, as in chapter 1, the Lord is one—there is but one body, as there is one Christ.

In chapter 12 the diversity within the body is set out. Diversity between members is ruled out as a ground for separating. It is actually just the reverse—the diversity of the members is the foundational strength of the body which should give it a unity which is not disrupted. The scriptural teaching here is simply that differences between the members of the body (whether of 'gifts', dispositions or preferences) should make them bind together all the more strongly. The church is not to divide into separate clone-like groupings where like companies with like, and only likes the company of the like. Jesus would say that this is the world's way of loving. If you love those who love you, or keep company with those who naturally would keep company with you, then you are producing a worldly, sect-like grouping—even if your agenda are religious activities like worship or Bible study or prayer.

It is, therefore, no mistake in Paul's structuring of his letter that chapter 13 follows chapter 12. The principle of the unlike members having need of each other for a harmony within the body is a very dynamic one. It is not simply a formal relationship of members that is sought. It is no less than a living, loving, harmonious pattern of corporate activity and mutual energizing which is in view. Love alone will bind the members—and 1 Corinthians 13 does not spare us in its demands.

This has implications for new converts. We find here a reinforcement of the picture I provided earlier—that the convert was converted through meeting persons who embodied the gospel (partly through their community life in love), and when he then received the good news he was baptized (with his family an Anglican would note). In that baptism he was reckoned as being received under the headship of Christ; brought within the saving power of Christ; grafted into the community, the body of Christ; and, if we care so to put it, he thus 'joined the church'.

It was all one step and he had no 'choice' about which congregation and its ways of worship would 'suit' him—although once within the church he might well play his part in helping implement Paul's instructions in, say, 1 Corinthians 14. Entry into the one church was part of his original submission to the gospel, and he could not raise questions about that.

We see this further worked out in the congregations implied by the letter to the Hebrews, 2 Peter, the Johannine letters, and the letters to the seven churches in Asia at the beginning of the Book of Revelation. In each case there is a very mixed kind of congregation—one including moral backsliders, doctrinally erroneous or at best dubious people, stiff-necked and petty persons, and sometimes strikingly wrong leaders. *But none of these scriptures tells the 'true believers' to pull out and found a new 'pure' church.* Rather the apostolic letters (scriptures) being sent to them are their best hope of reformation. Reform of doctrine and revitalization of life is to come from persons within the church applying the word of God lovingly (yet, if necessary, sternly) to the life of the church. Pulling out to found a new fellowship may, for the sake of the present argument, be deemed allowable in extreme cases—but if we so deem it, we have at the same time to acknowledge that it is not so revealed in the New Testament, which totally lacks any God-given precedent or command in this direction.

So what of the dear old Church of England?

How then does the present church situation in England measure up to these scriptural principles? We have to start with history. What claims, in the denominational chaos, does the original church of the land have in England?

One thing must be made clear. This *is* the same church as that which Augustine founded in Kent in 597 A.D. It had its ups and downs, and many internal frictions. It went the way of the medieval church generally, as it was all of a single piece with the papacy in Rome. But it witnessed to certain valuable principles, which have easily been forgotten today, or have presented themselves in such a guise within the Roman Catholic Church that they have not been widely recognized as valuable.

Firstly, it was an historic church. That is to say that it had had a visible and ancient life, in continuity with the planting (or replanting) of Christianity in Anglo-Saxon England. It had never split off from some greater body. It had never formed itself from scratch over and against an existing church. *It was the people of the land at prayer and worship*.

This is not particularly a claim to 'apostolic succession', though the ordered succession of bishops of various sees (e.g. Canterbury, London, Lichfield) undoubtedly helped witness to that continuity of church life which from the New Testament one would expect. (This is very seriously meant—even in the seven churches in Asia in Revelation 2–3 the few godly persons in somewhat corrupt, heretical, immoral or luke-warm congregations were never anywhere told to pull out and refound the church. Even in those circumstances the faithful were to 'hold fast' and persevere with existing church life, seeking to influence it from within, no doubt, but not leaving.)

Secondly, it was, of course, a connectionalist church. That is to say, there was a structure which was wider and firmer than the bonding together of individuals of any one particular locality into one independent congregation, and those of another into another independent congregation (or, worse, the forming of two congregations in the same place). While we know little of the ways in which congregations were bonded into a worldwide church in the New Testament, we can see that the congregations could not view themselves as autonomous under God but as interconnected with each other and interdependent upon each other. The role of the apostles gives one witness of this, and the Jerusalem Council in Acts 15 highlights this supervisory role. On a smaller scale the position of Titus in Crete, somewhat later, seems to have been not unlike that of a modern bishop!

The Church of England reflected this structure in its developed Roman style in the Middle Ages. While the shape of the papacy was no doubt erroneous, yet the principle of connectionalism was right, and was retained by the reformers. Anglicans practise it to this day, usually by a 'synodical' form of interdependence. It should be noted that such connectionalism is both pastoral and missionary—pastoral because it links and strengthens the Christians of a district, region, or nation; missionary because only a body with a care for that whole district, region or nation can properly see how and where best to plan a missionary strategy. Thus the parish system of the Church of England (while it has enormous anomalies in inherited boundaries) represents not simply a haphazard agreement by individual congregations not to get in each other's way, but also some overview and care which has attempted to respond to movements of population, to the development of new housing areas, and to an awareness of our weakness in many places—not by withdrawing from areas where Christians cannot support congregational life, but rather by putting resources in for missionary purposes.

In all this there is a genuine contrast here with independent congregations, for the tendency of Christians who club together on congregationalist principles is not only to have several competing congregations in areas of relatively strong Christianity, but also to have no strategy in relation to the areas of the church's weakness.

It might of course be objected that the logic of this is a worldwide 'connection' such as the structure of the Church of Rome displays. The logic has a certain appeal, and certainly the Jerusalem Council and the role of Paul in New Testament days had a 'whole world' (or *oikumene*) orientation. But there are grave problems of an organizational sort in a structure for the whole world, and the Anglican answer has corresponded (rightly or wrongly) to the way in which the erstwhile British Empire turned itself into a Commonwealth of nations. The Roman Catholic model of universal jurisdiction by the Pope (and thus by his secretariat) is not self-evidently the only possible method which could be explored for a single world-wide structure, but, as it is the only one which actually exists, it is bound to be under review. To an outsider it looks over-hierarchical, over-clerical, and with its central administration removed from the run of parish life. It should be noted that this latter problem is not true of the Church of England's central organization—clergy and laity from very ordinary parishes take their part in the life of the General Synod as the backbone of what the Synod actually is.

Thirdly, the Church of England has a concept of 'one church in each place'. There is a territorial way of understanding its role—an approach which runs very close to the two previous points. Its apparent sense of superiority towards other denominations in the land has arisen not only through the sins of actual individuals (which affect the stances of all churchly bodies), but also because in each place in the land— each town, each village—it claimed to be *the* church of the town or village, gathering all the inhabitants into one congregation in the days when the whole population was reckoned as Christian, and at least those who would see themselves as believers and worshippers in post-Christendom days. It treasures an ideal whereby all the believers in one street, or one block of flats, or one town square, know each other as believers, meet each other as such on Sundays, and together sustain a care for the sick and needy in that street, and look for opportunities for evangelism in it too. The ideal of one people of God, one body, one eucharistic fellowship, in each place is not only true to the pattern we have seen in 1 Corinthians, but is also well designed to exhibit a single loving community before the world's gaze in each place, and to undertake service there of the civic community and its needs on behalf of Jesus Christ.

This in turn has often made it difficult for Anglicans to respond mutually when others have offered 'recognition' to them. The Free Churches in England have, almost by definition, been committed to the view that Christians could, and sometimes should, separate from parent denominations; that they could then set up in Anglican parishes; and that they then could ask for full recognition as being part of the world-wide church. The Church of England has thus far given only qualified responses to this sort of presentation, and has often sounded as though its problem is bishops, or baptism, or the state connection. *But in fact the difficulties lie closer to the issue of abandoning a trusteeship for 'one church in each place'.*

However, difficulties in allocating an equal place to others as they are, are much reduced—perhaps even eliminated—if we can join together with them to pursue a united future. Sometimes a genuine merging of congregations must be sought (especially when weak congregations are busy duplicating each other's role and costs). In others a new distribution of territorial responsibility can be tried, for example, where a united congregation can be formed on a new housing estate, or an existing Methodist congregation in one part of an Anglican parish could be recognized as 'the' church in that area.

Fourthly, biblically-minded Christians are bound to ask why doctrine has not figured earlier in this explanation of the inner purpose of the Church of England. Largely, this is because I stand by my conviction that gathering a worshipping community is in many ways logically prior to its own confession of the faith—though it is certainly near to extinction if it cannot then confess the faith. People join the church by the simple profession 'Jesus is Lord', the New Testament baptismal profession. They need to be converted by this means into the community which is bonded by the same profession. They enter a tradition—a tradition of teaching. Anglicans will certainly have discovered this. They inherit formularies—whether the Thirty-Nine Articles or liturgical texts. But these represent a doctrinal witness, and a *prima facie* doctrinal position. They cannot be viewed as definitive for ever in the way the Scriptures are. The living church holds the Scriptures in its hands, and is in constant dialogue with its own inherited past.

This is the principle described by the reformers (who used a Latin tag for it) as 'the church once reformed is constantly up for further reform'. It means that doctrinal standards are not simply created once in history, and from then on are points of reference backwards—plumb-lines against which heresies can be measured out. This concept is understandable, and the ancient creeds have gone near to fulfilling that role. But doctrinal witness comes from an eschatological process also—as the church continues this dialogue with its past in changing contemporary conditions, so it refines and restates its doctrinal witness. As with moral perfection, it works on into the future to attain a fulfilment it has not yet got. Meantime its doctrine, like its morals, has a provisional kind of character to it, and the refinement continues. It is thus appropriate to appeal to the Thirty-Nine Articles as part of the evidence of how the Church of England has seen, yes and does see, its doctrinal position; but its current forms of worship, current declaration of assent, current emphases in preaching, the actual expression of its living spiritual life, these are all also important.

The church's doctrine is described as much as prescribed—but that is balanced by the prescriptive task of continuous reapplication of the scriptural message to the present day, and the prescriptive task of the living dialogue with the past from the scriptures, that the church may be reformed and revived for the future.

Of course, Anglicanism has terrible weaknesses. They can be admitted, rather than denied. But they will fit into the frame I have set out, rather than destroy it. So the wobbly Anglican, or would-be Anglican, can afford to be wholly realistic in his assessment—which would not always be true in other cases. The Church of England is in pilgrimage, with its eyes on heaven. It has a sequence to follow which includes sinners, muddled people, inadequate people, and every class and colour of person. This is the New Testament pattern, and no one need be ashamed to follow it.

4

ESTABLISHED TO SERVE THE NATION

by

*Timothy Hoare**

Mandell Creighton, Bishop of London at the turn of the century, once declared, 'I am not ashamed to own that I am an Englishman first and a Churchman afterwards. But to my mind Church and State are not contradictory things but the nation looked at from different points of view.' It is hard to imagine any bishop making such an assertion today, but for many centuries it was a commonly held view. The establishment of the Church of England used to be thought to rest upon two principles.

One of these was the identical membership of Church and State, although there had never been a time since the mid-sixteenth century when all English citizens had been members of the established Church. The growth of dissent and its increasing acceptance by the State had made Mandell Creighton's claim highly questionable by the twentieth century.

The other principle by which establishment was justified was the supremacy of the person of the monarch in the government of the Church, firmly replacing the rule of the

*Sir Timothy Hoare served on the staff of the Church Youth Fellowships Association and the Pathfinder Movement for some years before becoming a Director of Career Plan, a company providing vocational guidance and personnel services. He has been a member of the Standing Committee of General Synod since 1980 and served on the Chadwick Commission on Church and State. He lives in Islington with his wife and three teenage children.

Pope after the Reformation. The royal supremacy was carefully defined in Article 37 and was often exercised within a legal framework, through the Council and Parliament. It was characteristic of Elizabeth I that she could act vigorously and in personal terms towards the Church. To one bishop she wrote 'Proud prelate, you know what you were before I made you what you are now. If you do not immediately comply with my request, I will unfrock you, by God'.

Although the association between monarch and Church was clarified at the Reformation, the link can be traced throughout English history. A law of Edward the Confessor stated, 'The King, who is the Vicar of the highest King is ordained to this end, that he shall govern and rule the earthly Kingdom and the people of the Lord, and above all things the Holy Church, and that he defend the same from wrongdoers'. By the nineteenth century the personal sovereignty of the monarch had evolved into a constitutional monarchy, exercised through ministers and Parliament, and the position of the King or Queen as Supreme Governor of the Church had begun to look as anachronistic as had the claimed consensus of the membership of Church and State.

Strictly speaking, the establishment of a church refers to its recognition in law by the State. It is thought that the earliest reference to the Church of England as established occurs in an Act of Parliament in Edward III's reign (Dibden, *Establishment in England,* Macmillan). But it is typical of the British Constitution that there is no one Act of Parliament which formally establishes the Church. It was the dominant position of the church in the life of our nation since Saxon times, which inevitably led to its partnership with the State.

This development over such a long period of time has produced a complex but flexible relationship between Church and State in England. It has constantly evolved and responded to the new circumstances and challenges of each generation.

A major crisis occurred during the nineteenth century when it was realized that the twin pillars of establishment had lost much of their substance. Owen Chadwick's *Victorian*

Church (A & C Black) describes how national leaders began to set boundary posts for the points of change beyond which it would no longer be possible to call the Church established. Edward Stanley said 'It was of the very essence of the union of the Church and State that the State shall out of the public funds defray the expenses of the religion it establishes' (something that still occurs in some other European churches today). Peel and Wellington drew the line at the Anglican constitution of Oxford and Cambridge universities, which they saw as the strongest bond of Church and State. These boundary posts were removed long ago, but establishment remains.

Only as one takes an historical perspective does it become clear how adaptable the partnership has been. Many see this as its great strength. To others, who seek a separation of Church and State, it causes great frustration. They can see that in recent years the terms of the partnership have been modified to such an extent that our recent forebears might doubt if anything worthy of the name 'establishment' is now left. Successive Commissions on Church and State during this century have noted this, marvelling that the relationship of Church and State has been preserved through so many changes in society. The consensus of their reports has been that it is not for the Church to call for disestablishment unless its essential life and witness are jeopardized. They have sought rather to seek to persuade the State to agree to alter the legal expression of the partnership in certain areas of church life.

Notable changes have been made. For many years some churchmen looked enviously at the form of establishment in Scotland, which for historical and theological reasons made that Church less obviously subject to control by the Crown, especially in the appointment of its chief officers and in the ordering of its doctrine and worship. The Church of England can now claim a similar measure of authority over these matters. The General Synod exercises effective control over doctrine and worship and elected representatives of the Church participate in the selection of names from which the

Crown, on the advice of the Prime Minister, appoints bishops. This latest adjustment is still on trial, so to speak. It seems to meet the requirement that the whole Church should play a formal role in the choice of its leaders, while also retaining the constitutional proprieties that the Monarch should be seen to make the final choice. Those who dislike the continuing part of the Prime Minister on the grounds that he or she may be personally disinterested in or antagonistic to Christianity, or may seek to gain political influence through particular nominations to the Bench, must suggest further modifications which would be acceptable constitutionally.

Neither the Queen nor the Prime Minister can be treated as rubber stamps. Yet, as has been noted above, the forms of our establishment have shown a remarkable capacity for change and a further lessening of the role of the Prime Minister in Crown Appointments may not be out of the question. It is worth recalling that under the present arrangements, however, there are several checks against abuse. The Prime Minister is subject to public opinion, is limited to ordained Anglican priests who have been chosen by the Church's own selection process, and, at the end of the day, the Church's seal on the selection has to be given in the bishop's consecration. On the positive side it should be added that bishops are still national figures; and it is proper for there to be wide-ranging enquiries about suitable candidates, enquiries conducted by both Church and State. Indeed, by comparison with the sometimes contentious election of bishops in other provinces of the Anglican Communion, our Crown appointment system has much to commend it.

There are other arguments used against the establishment of the Church of England. It is seen sometimes as an archaic relic of the days when bishops were 'princes' in the land. Some judge that in the minds of many people, particularly the deprived, alienated or less privileged, establishment inevitably puts the Church on the side of 'them' and against 'us'. They perceive the Church, it is said, as part of the wealthy, ruling class, the 'establishment', and that this can be a major handicap to its mission. That there is truth in this claim cannot be denied, but it is not due solely—or even mainly—to the Church's links with the State. Disestablishment alone would not necessarily destroy the Church's middle-class aura of respectability, as a glance at the Episcopal Churches of North America seems to confirm.

Apart from the residual endowments held by the Church Commissioners and the right to use cathedrals and parish churches, the Church of England receives no obvious material benefit from its establishment. It is true that the Church might redirect more of its resources to the needs of mission in the inner cities (as the recent report, *Faith in the City* recommends), but that report and the strongly radical trend of opinion in the Church hardly conveys the impression of a Church which is a bastion of privilege or the 'establishment' class. The fact that it is usually Tory M.P.s who fall over themselves in a rush to profess to be outraged by Church statements, may indicate that the Church is 'on course' on social questions more often than off it! In the nature of things, an established church is bound to have close links with the influential in the land. The question to be asked, surely, is not how can we cut those links, but how can we best use them for the gospel?

It is sometimes said against establishment that it requires a complex form of government in the Church, forcing the General Synod to act as a quasi sub-committee of Parliament. In fact all churches are subject to the law and decision-making in other denominations is not significantly more speedy or representative than that of the Church of England.

It is also argued that the establishment is a barrier to reunion between the Christian churches in this country. Certainly there may have been truth in that in the past, although most of the evidence given to the Chadwick Commission on Church and State indicated that the objections of the other churches lay not so much with the principle of establishment as with certain aspects of it—Parliamentary control of worship and doctrine and the method of Crown Appointments. Subsequent modifications in these areas may well have made establishment less offensive, although of course, full reunion remains a hypothetical question and many are thinking now of a loose federation of churches rather than one mammoth denomination. Many Christian leaders recognize the benefits to the Christian cause in England to be gained from the association of the State with a Christian church.

A further argument against establishment (although it can be used against all churches too) is that public status and position can dull its missionary zeal. People point to the Church Commissioners and accuse the Church of living off the past. In fact, its inherited wealth is making a rapidly diminishing contribution to the payment of the clergy. In 1979 the 'living church' contributed 24% of stipends, in 1985 it was expected to be 44%. We seem to be moving in the right direction. Disendowment, which would in some degree accompany disestablishment, would in the short term seriously impede the Church's task of taking the Good News of Christ to every person in England. Some feel, nevertheless, that the drastic step is needed to wake Church people from their slumber. The evidence, however, from churches which have experienced disestablishment is that revival does not necessarily result! A better way is to pray and to teach the responsibility of Christian discipleship and spirituality.

If we can no longer support a Church-State relationship on the twin pillars of automatic identity of membership of the two and the personal role of the monarch—where can we look for a better basis? What would give us a positive justification for keeping the link in place?

There are two important, if pragmatic, arguments. Both relate to the Church's responsibility to the whole nation.

Reference is often made to the privileges of the Church of England. The Archbishop crowns the Sovereign, who must be a member of the Church of England. Bishops sit in Parliament. Chaplains are appointed (at the State's expense) to hospitals and prisons; and so one could continue. But looked at from another angle, these privileges are also opportunities for service. They form part of the general task of the Church to provide for the spiritual needs of the nation. The statement of the National Evangelical Anglican Congress in 1977 put it well:

> We hope that our church will not seek to renounce, but to share with other Protestant churches the ancient constitutional ties that establish her as the church of this realm. We value these not for privilege but for service, not for the church but for the nation. We look beyond the secularism of the present to a day when the English people shall again seek the substance as well as the name of Christian faith.

One application of this principle of service to the nation can be seen in the present requirement for a parish priest to conduct the marriage of any parishioner (unless previously divorced). Some clergy find this an unacceptable duty, perhaps with some reason if the person happens to deny the Christian faith. But the basis of this provision, and many other practical expressions of establishment, spring from the ideal of missionary concern and pastoral care. The parochial system expresses this legally as well as geographically

> because the visiting opportunities that one has in a parish are unique in the English situation and must be exploited for the Gospel. In America, for instance, no-one has the right to knock on every door and call indiscriminately and the Episcopalian clergyman would be out of order if he did so. In England, however, the people have a subconscious feeling that the Church of England ought to be interested and concerned for their well-being. (*Like a Mighty Army*, M. A. P. Wood.)

The opportunity to minister to everyone in his parish brings the vicar face to face with the question of how he is to treat the fringe members of the church, and in particular with their 'folk religion'. His response to requests to baptize, marry and bury his parishioners will vary greatly as the following letters in *The Times* well demonstrate:

> Vast numbers of loyal Anglicans remain worried, distressed and concerned at our undisciplined administration of the sacraments— Holy Communion as well as baptism and matrimony—and the ultra-establishment attitude which accepts and even encourages the absurd, and ultimately blasphemous, status of the 'occasional

churchgoer'. The New Testament knows nothing of the occasionally committed disciple. All of which is symptomatic of the spiritual anaemia growing out of establishment. (Canon Martin Thornton, September 9th 1985.)

I find the narrowness of your correspondent, with his talk of the blasphemous status of the 'occasional churchgoer', both frightening and horrifying, and yet it is the sort of attitude I would expect to develop were disestablishment to take place. The Church of England has the duty and privilege of ministering to all the people of this country as they need it. As much as the regular churchgoers, this includes those who feel the need to worship only at the great festivals, or at times of stress or joy in their lives, when we bury them in sympathy and love, and marry them in joy. It also has the duty to be a great safety net for those who never come, and to be there just in case they should need its help. This seems to be the only way for the Church to serve the world as the Body of Christ. (The Rev. Michael Burke, October 11th 1985.)

These divergent opinions are held widely in the Church, and represent what Bruce Reed (*Dynamics of Religion*, Darton, Longman and Todd) calls the 'associational' and 'communal' models of the church. The establishment has tended to draw the Church of England to the second of these, with its concern to embrace a wide spectrum of faith without requiring too strict a commitment from those to whom it is willing to minister. For some, like Canon Thornton, that is its major weakness. They include many evangelicals who identify easily with the gathered church which was suited to the circumstances in which the New Testament church developed. Others who support the communal church model, of which the Church of England has been a notable example, look to the Old Testament—one nation under God, led by a godly prince—or to the many churches which, since the conversion of Constantine, have lived in partnership with the secular rulers.

In England today a persuasive case can be made for either model. The strategy which one prefers may depend upon one's own temperament and philosophy as much as upon an understanding of the evidence of the Bible or the sociologists.

Advocates of the establishment pray that through evangelistic and pastoral opportunities 'occasional churchgoers' will be revitalized by the Holy Spirit. Although it is dangerous to generalize about the spiritual health of the nation, *they judge that our people are not self-evidently pagan or anti-Christian, in the way it was possible to describe those Gentiles to whom the Apostles first preached.* Indeed had England's spiritual tone declined that far, it would have been reflected in Parliament, leading to demands for disestablishment from the State.

As it is, both the statistics of church attendance and surveys of opinions on religious questions indicate that while our country is in no sense in a religious revival, people in many areas are open to the gospel. A 1982 survey by the Bible Society found that 64% declared themselves to be adherents of the Church of England. Certainly there are dark areas; the report *Faith in the City* speaks of attendance at Anglican inner city churches of less than 1%. 'From a sociological perspective, active churchgoers form the tip of a huge religious iceberg. They are simply the most visible and articulate part of a much more widespread phenomenon'. (J. Habgood, *Church and Nation*, Darton, Longman and Todd.) Disestablishment, far from awaking the Church, might turn it in on itself and away from the task of bringing the 'submerged' to real faith in Christ and commitment to discipleship. It could remove the challenge, ever-present to a national church, to minister to the whole nation.

The other pragmatic justification for establishment today can be drawn from a consideration of the benefits which a Christian understands the State to receive from an association with the Church. In *The Functions of a National Church* (Latimer House, Ed. R. Johnson) Max Warren describes the Church's duty; to remind the State that it is responsible to God, to seek to purify the State of its tendency to be corrupted by power, and to prepare the nation for judgement and the coming of the kingdom of God. A reviewer commented that these responsibilities fall to any church, established or not. But the point is that in England the national established Church traditionally had, and still has, platforms provided for its work towards the State.

Church spokesmen frequently contribute to discussion of public affairs and are heard as representatives of the national Church. One could wish that more often they would address directly the issues mentioned by Max Warren. In our particular spiritual situation in England, bishops, for example, could make more of their opportunities to take on the mantle of evangelist and declare the gospel of Christ plainly, outside church settings. 'Pre-eminently the bishop was a missionary, pressing on into new territory, encountering new principalities and powers, and leaving behind him (unless he were martyred!) 'churches' and 'parishes'. (E. R. Wickham, former Bishop of Middleton, in *The English Church*, Penguin.)

The nation and its leaders need reminding forcibly of the inadequacy of any materialistic philosophy, the ultimate rule of God and the saving power of Christ. We have had several vivid warnings this century of what happens to a nation if Christian leaders fail to speak the word of God. We can thank God that many political leaders still welcome a clear spiritual lead and expect the Church to use the facilities which are provided by establishment. As the powers of central government increase, it is more than ever necessary for the Church to exercise its prophetic role, reminding the State, in the words of the Chadwick Commission, 'that it is one of God's instruments; that moral laws apply to it; that it has a duty to encourage the good when it can do so expediently, and discourage the bad.'

Christianity remains the principal source of moral and ethical guidance for the nation. Although we can be justly proud of what has been achieved (often on the initiative of Christians) in terms of humanitarian care and compassion for the needy, vigilance is needed to preserve it. We must accept that the Established Church has a rather mixed record on social reform: bishops in the Lords often led the opposition to change in the nineteenth century. Today, however, the Church's concern for the problems of the deprived is a much needed antidote to the rapid growth of vehement self-interest in many sections of society. The Church of England, through its public recognition, has opportunities at every level of our national life to apply this antidote of the love and justice of Christ for those in need.

The Established Church also has a contribution towards the maintenance of national unity. In our fragmented and pluralistic society, many look to the monarchy as a symbol that still has power to unite the nation. Without being too mystical, the visible and close relationship of the sovereign with the Church must reinforce and enhance the force of that symbol, reminding all that rulers hold their authority from God. Many people, perhaps unconsciously, recognize this. A 1984 Gallup Poll showed that 83% of the population favoured the Queen remaining Supreme Governor of the Church of England.

The established status of the Church of England compels the State to take note of it. A State in which the Church is established cannot be neutral towards the claims of Christianity. It was said earlier that those who wish to preserve the Church-State partnership do so in the expectation of a revitalization of the nation's faith. If the reverse happens then the State would disestablish the Church as part of a national rejection of Christian truth and standards. But this chapter has argued that this seems not to be imminent in England today. There is still mileage in an establishment whose terms are subject to examination and revision and which is used by the Church as a basis for service to the whole nation. The strategy for mission given by Christ to his disciples in Matthew 10 suggests that so long as people are willing to receive his messengers, they should remain there and preach and minister to them. Likewise, while the State is prepared to give the Church of England a recognition, expressed through forms which we call establishment, it is not for the Church to seek to withdraw from it.

The Christian gospel, however, has a very strongly intolerant or exclusive streak ('God commands all men everywhere to repent') and as Christ warns in Matthew 10, persecution (in place of recognition) by secular authorities could well follow if the nation really does decide to try to be neutral on religious matters; for such neutrality is really rejection of the claims of Christ and cannot be compatible with the establishment of a Christian church.

No blueprint is provided in the Bible for the relationship of Church and State. Each generation of Christians must accept, discern and adapt what they receive which is what the Church of England is engaged in doing. Perhaps the problem of finding the ideal relationship between any church and any state 'will never be solved until the coming of the Son of Man, when there shall be no King but Christ and all nations, people and languages shall bow down before Him' (Browne, on Article 37).

PART TWO

The Task

5

DOWN BY THE RIVERSIDE

by

*Christopher Idle**

It is three in the morning. I am sitting in the vestry, a little chilly since it is November. Time for more coffee, then another prowl round the churchyard with my torch.

Yesterday was Sunday: a lovely day, as Sundays usually are. In the morning the heaters were working, and we used our new communion service for the first time—a local version of the nearest thing we have to a modernized Prayer Book liturgy. In the evening, two car-loads of us went through the Rotherhithe Tunnel to the Old Kent Road for a guest service; that left about fifteen to worship here, and God was with us all.

So what am I doing here? Good question. Immediately, I am defending this massive piece of masonry they call our church from the lead-thieves who called a few nights back. The roof-high scaffolding makes things easier for them; yesterday the scaffolders arrived early to remove the top layers they had finished with—to make it safer. I had told them to clear off because it was Sunday; so until they clocked in on Monday morning, I felt a bit responsible.

---

*Christopher (Chris) Idle graduated from Oxford with a degree in English. His entire ministry has been concentrated in urban areas with eighteen years in inner London parishes. He is at present Rector of Limehouse where the parish church building (Hawksmoor 1730) is the oldest and finest structure in the neighbourhood. Chris ministers in a multi-racial area, writes superb hymns, does twelve-mile runs, supports CND and tries to be a good husband and father to his wife and four sons.

Why me, and not someone else? If you ask that question, you cannot be in the inner-city. Nor in the heart of the country either, I suspect, but in the grey shadowlands between. It's a matter of recognizing available gifts: this is one of mine. (I was painting the lettering on our notice-board once, and a passing member of the Christian Brethren said 'Haven't you got any minions who can do that?' Alas no— only brothers and sisters! But his assembly is in Wales; there are none here.)

In the longer term, my presence here is harder to explain. Part of being a Church of England clergyman seems to be looking after half the nation's ancient monuments; this one happens to be on the large side. One friend seeing it for the first time said 'Couldn't you let it down a bit?' On nights like these I think wistfully of Baptist or Mission-Hall colleagues who do not get sidetracked into such occupations as mine. If God calls me to preach his word, why am I here?

Escape?

For other reasons too I sometimes long to escape. We pursue a policy on baptism which some find rigidly exclusive, others weakly compromising. 'Outsiders' want baptism and nothing less; they don't usually get it. 'Insiders' are urged to have it, and often don't want it. So many things Anglican leave much to be desired: O for the wings of a dove, to fly away into the ideal and perfectly-purified church!

In too many groups I am in an odd minority. Among fellow-Anglicans, a naive 'fundamentalist' whose presence is desired at annual 'unity' services but whose Protestantism is greeted with amused incredulity for the rest of the year. Among free church friends, a brother indeed, but often on the defensive over bishops, Lent, or Christian initiation—let alone robes, titles, and parish boundaries.

John Newton, the 18th-century slave-trader turned hymn-writer, who also in his latter years had a Hawksmoor building to enjoy, was a kindred spirit. 'I am a mighty good Churchman', he wrote to William Bull, 'but I pass among such as a

Dissenter *in prunello* [in other plumage?]. On the other hand, the Dissenters think me defective, either in understanding or in conscience, for staying where I am. Well, there is a middle party called the Methodists, but neither do my dimensions exactly fit with them.'

My closest friend among modern Methodists argues for staying put whatever your dimensions. The church is in such a mess, he says, and over its 2,000 years has probably done more harm than good. Wesley reckoned you could go to hell from any denomination; you may change persuasions, but you change nothing else. So my friend will die (but not go to hell) a Methodist; we stay on opposite sides, meanwhile, of this fairly low earthly fence. But is that all there is to say in favour of standing firm?

To return to our buildings: we did not choose their size, or shape, or location. But we have heard more stories of bondage to them while they stand, than of liberation from them when they fall. We do not escape by altering our affiliation.

When one of the 'Operation Mobilisation' ships berthed in our nearby dock, part of its tourist attraction was a descent to the boiler-room. It showed, as I recall, the power of God. Our church boiler seems to me as big a miracle as any, but I confess that it is not yet on our visitors' itinerary. I discover, too, that URCs have leaky roofs, and 'Fellowships' who hire halls and warehouses constantly make their premises a matter for prayer.

One summer our family went to Butlins at Barry Island. After a Sunday morning service on site, we chose to escape to a 'real' church in the evening. How to find one, with little time and no transport? It was easy: over there, and there, and there, were buildings that *looked* like houses of Christian prayer; they had spires or towers! The nearest one proved just right; were they so wrong to build such an identifiable home? And all through the year, hesitant souls venture over our own threshold because they can see where we meet—or even hear our bell.

Christians who move into anonymous or neutral accommodation often find it makes no difference to growth; in spite of volumes written to assert the contrary, evangelism or the lack of it is governed by factors quite other than architecture. What a building 'says' to a community varies as widely as the listeners. The difference made to a district by its parish church can be appreciated only when you lock the door for the last time. I have done that too; by then it is too late.

In ten years at Limehouse we have come through fire and flood; the fires seemed worse than the floods, though even they brought their blessings. To have a serious conflagration in two opposite corners of the nave, halted after an hour thanks to one alert neighbour and some prompt firemen: nearly to lose our thunderous organ and much else with it: this makes anyone wary of claiming that other people's fires are judgements from heaven. Floods (judgements, sometimes, in the past) are less spectacular but more insidious; there is no flood brigade to soak up the lakes of brown pigeon-smelling rainwater oozing oilily across the carpet.

Such events, such buildings, will not argue me out of the Church of England; not even tonight. If this structure had never been built, you would not be reading this page; nor would I be praying and preaching here; nor would anyone else.

On offer

For what can Limehouse at this moment offer the seeker after God, or those who are not seeking but who must be sought? Not a great deal. As in many London parishes, Roman Catholics are evidently present; so, just about, is the London City Mission, still unsure if it is a church or not. So is one other minute Christian group, supported by resources far more remote than any Church Commissioner, and almost defunct, but occupying superb modern street-level premises in the main shopping area. So much for those who believe that plant is the key factor. Methodists, Baptists, URC, Salvation Army, have all been, and all gone; they are within a bus ride, but they are not here.

Two miles west in Spitalfields the contrast is even clearer. For Protestants, the choice is Christ Church (C. of E.) or nothing. Or indeed do what many city Christians do, and join the Sunday commuters to a favourite fellowship well outside the neighbourhood. Rector Eddy Stride is emphatic that in that parish, no Church of England would mean no biblical gospel. The house church theory did not work there, and never had; with all our blemishes, Anglicans had been there throughout the three centuries since the community grew up.

So how does our own church serve the people of the parish? Certainly at those root experiences of birth, marriage, and death. For us, death has sometimes dominated—in church, school, and family. Cancer has claimed more than one Christian leader in the prime of life, and the shock-waves throb far beyond the signed-up membership. When the community weeps, and when it sees a weeping church, there is a precious moment of communication that cannot be encapsulated in a tract or a text.

Marriages?—not very many. In spite of having a lively and gifted group of marriageable Christians, hardly any church members have married one another here. There are lessons in this; in the plummeting statistics of non-members who ask for a church wedding; and in the fact that there are whole blocks, whole streets, with hardly one straightforward married relationship in evidence.

There has been birth; many natural babies, and some spiritual ones from around seven years old to over seventy. Births often bring problems; we praise God for every sign of struggling new life. Some of our newborn experiments as a church win through to toddlerhood, even maturity; a few are worth a closer look.

Students

Let us start with students. We now have so many that you cannot help bumping into a group of them round the coffee-hatch on Sunday mornings. So many, compared not with the declared 'student-churches', but with how it used to be. We have never set out to attract them, though more and more now have inner-city accommodation. Before they began to congregate here, we forged a link between the church and one college Christian Union. Every year a small group (from two to six) came for a long week and divided their time between study, practical jobs (cleaning, painting, repairing), and some pastoral/evangelistic ministry. It might include planning and leading a service, midweek meetings, school assemblies, youth groups, and a variety of parish happenings. The student week became something of an institution; after eight years it came to an end, partly because we were thinking too much about college life, not enough about urban realities.

But we were all learning, and there were other unlooked-for gains. Three of those who first came for a week returned and stayed on for years after graduating. One was ordained; another used his practical skills to good effect before departing; the third thoughtfully married a wife, became our treasurer, and with his family added incalculably to the range of gifts entrusted to us. They also hosted another home-grown project: The Limehouse 'Think Tank'.

Think Tank

Today's church is faced with a whole battery of issues on which it is called to make decisions, or at least pronouncements. It is like an escalator ride; there isn't time to read all the adverts on the way up. You may not want to anyway; and none of them (you feel) are your main business.

It may always have been so; but creeping democracy in the church, changing views in society, better or faster means of communication—all these make for a fuller-than-ever agenda. Who has the time to tackle it? Ethical, social, political questions can hardly be left to the clergy!

We begrudged diverting the time set apart for prayer and the Scriptures into debates on abortion, racism, or women's ordination. Many such topics meet us head-on in Old Testament or New; but we needed more background documents, more time for study. The PCC could hardly weigh down its own programme too often with such questions.

So after a brief labour our Think Tank was born; a

quarterly date where a dozen of us do some homework on controverted topics, led by someone who had tried to digest a book, a crucial report, and a bit of history as well as the Bible background. Thought and talk sometimes lead to action; with members on all levels of the synodical system from local (deanery) to national (the General Synod), it has helped some of us to be better primed before launching out more widely—and to prime others in turn.

Leadership

Many parishes now have eldership teams, or some other recognized group of non-ordained local leaders. Some have written up their awesome successes in fair detail. We have to say we have not yet found the right formula here—but not for lack of trying. Why did our own 'Pastoral Team' run into the ground after three or four years?

Our experiment began when it became clear that we could not replace a former woman parish worker. Several of our members (at the time, all men) had received some training for Christian leadership. Their great differences in temperament could have been a strength. Spurred on by PCC, Area Dean, and Bishop, we began to meet, and to minister. But we did a lot more meeting than ministering! I knew the theory behind that; but to commit so many full evenings for so little output in terms of human availability—that was unbearable. I still recognize the potential of that group; we even grew, and added a woman! But as it folded, I began to see that we should have been looking not so much at past training and qualifications, but present gifts matching clear needs. And even from a gifted group, to choose people able and willing to make time to let in-group learning flow out much more widely; even to help me to be more effective as overall leader.

Sometimes this has looked like the ordinands' graveyard. As I write, we are well on the way to seeing our second former member (neither from inner-London) ordained; but too many others (some from inner-London) have seen their stirrings of what seemed God's call fade away in the face of various contrary factors.

Missionaries

For most of one year, though, we did have a rather different mini-team; here is something we *can* recommend! It took some desperate house-hunting, some urgent prayer, and some late, late decisions of faith, before we found a temporary home for a missionary family while they worshipped and worked with us. It was a redundant vicarage two miles away; just near enough. David and Helen Hazlewood's 'home' is Indonesia, where they serve with the Overseas Missionary Fellowship; after ten years abroad, this was their second furlough. They chose an urban base.

Like others before them, they found more blatant godlessness than last time, faster driving, and some relief from the rather different problems of Sumatran Christians. Parents and children, they enriched us greatly, steering us through a valuable study-course on Mission, and giving us the impetus to form four home-groups meeting in different local flats.

Yes, others had reached this point long before; but sometimes a new face and voice can achieve what more familiar ones cannot—or do it rather better. Not that these were exactly strangers; we had sent them off in 1976 and recommissioned them in 1980, since before their marriage Helen had belonged with us. But in five years the church population shifts, so now for some they were almost unknown except through letters, photos, and prayer.

So that year brought many pluses. But the hassle over their house still sticks in the brain; was it not the 'Fenton Morley Report' two decades ago which proposed that clergy overseas could stay 'On the books' of a home diocese even while they were not 'On the strength'? It alarmed me that their problem—where to live for nine months—seemed to be nobody else's responsibility; that surely needs attention.

Worship

David Sheppard, now Bishop of Liverpool, has often pleaded for worship to have both excitement and content. In *Built as a City* (1974) he says: 'I value a set Liturgy because I am no poet. Especially when it comes to praising God, I am thankful that I can use some of the treasures other men of God with greater abilities have given us both in prayers, in psalms and hymns. Liturgy, rightly used, can help to draw a congregation more fully to participate in worship than an entirely free service where so much depends on one man' (p.328). So in our worship, like many others, we have explored some varied styles and moods while retaining our Anglican roots and observing Anglican rules. Some might still find our 'average' service a bit heavy; others could think that we verged on flippancy. We have helped to launch a varied selection of new (brand new) hymns and songs, some of which have changed shape as a result, and some scrapped! We have had question-times with the sermon, drama and humour, and worshipped in the choir, both aisles, the crypt and the west porch, as well as our normal places. The porch is domed and circular, with room for thirty at a service or fifty for a party; the crypt, hollowed out two years ago from the old burial vaults, has also seen 'church family lunches' followed by a frame or two of community snooker and other relaxations. But preaching the word is paramount; this has included a series of 66 sermons expounding and applying one Bible book at a time, with worship to match. To reach 'Revelation' was quite an experience!

Youth

The Church of England still believes that the body of Christ is not an adults-only society. That is part of the point of infant baptism; babies, children, and teenagers are not 'tomorrow's church' but today's. Our Pathfinders, Explorers, and other junior groups have seldom lacked committed leaders, and that is a rare privilege among urban churches. Harder to find, anywhere, are the skills needed for reaching the unclubbable youngsters who leave school with no paper qualifications, hardly open a book again, and head straight for the dole queue.

How do we cope with the merry rioters among them who get their laughs by disrupting Evening Prayer on Sundays? The first thing that struck me, literally, as I emerged through the big red door after a moving 'Carols by Candlelight' was a silver ball from the Christmas tree which they had just stripped and uprooted from its tub. (They had nicked a few presents and screwed up a few cards too.) There are worse things to throw—like darts—and some have graduated from glue to butane gas as the latest sniffable substance. A pound a day of somebody's money to add to the cigarette bill, and a churchyard littered with empty canisters.

David Sheppard again, when told years ago that he would never do any good with such kids: 'You either believe in redemption or you don't: I do.' And what little progress has been made, or is likely to be made, in any truly open youth work, seems to need a local church of local Christians more than anything else. This latest group know where I live, and they share their chips when we meet by the shops.

And since time has moved on since this chapter started, it is now Tuesday evening and the lead-thieves stayed away; the roof is pronounced 'safe'. The teenagers are round again, and when they tire of less exciting things (since concentration lasts about two minutes) we have a special attraction tonight: a visit underground to the church boiler! Yes, we can do it too.

Untold stories

And how I would love to write about Fred, and Rose, and Lily, and Alan . . . it is not only space that forbids it. In this most amazing of jobs, I sometimes get home after the events of a single day that would fill an enthralling book: miracles of God's grace to exhilarate heaven's angels and give his earthly saints the grit to battle on—or tragedies to make earth and heaven weep. But such stories are probably for pastor and people alone, not to spread before a sensation-loving world. Everyone can see the difference made by Christ; but only if their eyes are opened by the Holy Spirit of God.

Two fellowships

So there are some advances, some setbacks, of the kingdom

in London. What, I wonder, are my neighbours up to—the churches around us? When Howell Harris, leader in the 18th-century revival in Wales, was looked at askance for staying with the Anglicans, he found much cause for rejoicing still. 'I recommend the peaceable spirit that remains still in the established church, which tolerates such as differ from it, and does not quench this small beginning of a revival in it. I find the Lord's presence in the worship and ordinances, and I have great freedom to wrestle in prayer for it, and a strong confidence that God would receive and revive this work in it'. He goes on to disclaim any prejudice against any other 'party'; are we still at peace today, or is there prejudice on either side?

I belong to two groups of local Christian leaders. Both meet regularly; both are among my priorities. In one, a kind of evangelical fraternal where I happen to be the only Anglican, it is a privilege to be trusted by my more puritan brothers—it is all-male too—in spite of my establishment trappings. I share their prayers, their coffee, their news, their stimulation; their laughter at many things, but their deadly seriousness about the gospel of Jesus Christ. I come away, usually, uplifted by our combined intercession and praise, maybe remembering a text which had spoken to a fellow-pastor that week.

These keen and loving Dissenters would not easily cope with the wider face of Anglicanism which sometimes begins to resemble 'a unitarian, sodomite, and humanist church'—to quote not one of them but one of us. But we few can at least agree on the Scriptures and the way of salvation; we talk the same language, pray for conversions, engage in evangelism, and praise our recognizably risen Lord. The differences surface only when I don't know the latest songs they have picked up from somewhere, when they report the seemingly endless stream of baptisms in their churches, or when they occasionally pray for a church to be planted in some neighbouring parish. 'There is nothing' they say, 'between the river and the railway: maybe God will raise up a church there!'

That redoubtable Baptist C. H. Spurgeon once said 'The worst of it is, the growth of sacramentalism in the Established

Church is not like that of the mistletoe or a fungus upon an oak, it is a real and legitimate branch of the parent stem.' He thought the High Church party more consistent with the Prayer Book: 'It is true that the Articles are against them, but what are the Articles? They are read over perhaps once in a lifetime. The mischief is in the Catechism and the service book which are in constant use.' When, he asked, would the Prayer Book be revised?

If my praying friends are strongly Spurgeonite at these points, it does not seem to interrupt our fellowship or our prayer. In any case, they would put things differently today; and while there might be more to be said on behalf of the 39 Articles, the less said about the way we have revised the Prayer Book, the better.

Such is the Friday meeting; on Tuesday it is a different matter. Here is the (Anglican) Chapter Meeting of clergy and other parish staff in the Deanery. By way of contrast, I emerge from the smoke-choked premises of St Benedict's frustrated and cross. Our energies have been absorbed by money, administration, or maintenance. The temperature rises when we discuss funeral and cemetery rotas; we also get regular broadsides from the Social Responsibility lobby, that we have failed to help this or that needy group in east London. If as occasionally happens we debate theology, evangelicals are put firmly in their place, or our irrelevance is assumed. When I raised with a visiting speaker his use of the word 'fundamentalist' in widely different senses, his answer was that he didn't expect to meet someone like me at a meeting like this.

Friday, and Tuesday; no doubt which of the gatherings I have enjoyed the most. Part of my annoyance with the second meeting is at my own failure to express more clearly and effectively the biblical fundamentals which are so often by-passed or shrouded in mist. But I also have to ask: suppose there was no such meeting? How would the church and its leaders fare on a diet of Protestant piety alone?

It is easy for evangelicals to agree across the denomina-tional board on items which are not at the time causing any testing problems. But start working together as one church, try even to approximate to the common life of New Testament Christians within one area, and our loving agreement could be in trouble. And while I am humbled by the spiritual zeal of my like-minded brethren who believe their Bibles, I am also humbled and taught by the wide-ranging vision and work of those whose training, philosophy, and goals are miles away from mine. I have to learn not to assess the worth of an opinion or a ministry by the style of someone's dress, a different range of vocabulary, or the number of stubs in the ashtray.

Yes, I believe I would miss those ghastly meetings; and there is more to add. Many zealous free churchmen have acquired their own clutter of non-biblical luggage by way of titles, customs and rules. Many have scarcely begun to question the accepted role of women in the lifestyle of their churches or in the language they use; many are unaware of the racist dimension to our leadership patterns; and I meet none of them at borough-wide consultations for racial harmony, nor at city-wide protests against our willingness to use nuclear weapons.

'But they preach the word from the Scriptures!' Yes; and often with more confidence and power than I do; they dare to spend time on the sermon, and are blessed in doing it. But not always. A former Baptist neighbour told me he had preached about the Falklands war. 'What did you say?' 'Well, I showed them the Christian tradition of the Just War through history, and how our Task Force fitted that tradition because they were fighting for justice!' And if Argentinian Baptists disagreed? More evidence of their political conditioning and consequent moral blindness!

I am glad he mentioned tradition and history; here are two factors we must learn to assess positively and theologically. But I suspect they did not often feature in his sermons, except here when he took the unusual role of an Erastian chaplain to the government.

Should I question further that desire to set up 'churches' in allegedly unchurched tracts of London? You may think the existing church is compromised, sick, or even dead; but there is actually a church there. The biblical way is surely not to set up a better church beside it, but to pray and work for the healing, repentance, or revival of the one that is there. That is a man-and-woman-sized job!

Such tensions leave me with John Newton's dilemma, out of step with both groups of friends and fellow-pilgrims. But there is a more hopeful way of viewing it. Michael Saward has claimed, with much coherence, that evangelical Anglicans are near the very centre of the spectrum of differing traditions. Among the free churches, dare we hope to interpret our Anglican colleagues in a more helpful light? Among Anglicans, or even Romans, can we sometimes persuade them not to ignore the Baptists or the house-churches?

Unity schemes mainly feature groups with a less than clear-cut doctrine, or who are already in decline, rather than those which are both confident and growing. I have to remind my brother-clergy that those on the theological left (or is it right?) are here among us and often in good heart. We all are the body of Christ!

And there are further ways in which Anglicans score. The clergy stick around longer. Trainee journalists are told to get to know the vicar, not because he is all-wise or has a sensational story, but because he knows a great many people and may have been inside more homes than anyone except the meter-reader.

The current average stay for incumbents in Tower Hamlets is a dozen years; if that is nearly twice the national average (it must be the air—they have even begun to retire here) it is also well up on Free Church and Roman Catholic clergy. City Missionaries and Salvation Army staff move on with bewildering speed; committed nonconformists stay a little longer. It is not merely stagnation which gives the Church of England an unequalled record of consistent pastoral care.

Earlier this century, the Methodist William Lax stayed forty years in Poplar and became Mayor; he boasted that he had outlasted all the publicans on his patch. But even he moved to Blackheath before he retired, and his heirs have not approached his record.

And if our Anglican 'chapters' are an embarrassingly mixed bag, could that be a blessing rather than a blemish? If I were ever to join another persuasion (if they would have me), I would be nervous of their subtle and unspoken pressures to conform to group norms—pressures from which the Church of England is usually free. One of our glories is to recognize and welcome an enormous range of human personality and temperament; even more important for laity than for clergy. What Archbishop Runcie calls our 'reluctance to exclude anyone' no doubt sometimes goes too far. Extremes of looseness prevent true discipline; but at least in the cities, while no one parish church includes every facet of need, there is likely to be one within reach for you, whoever you may be.

Those who split off in the past, and those who may go their own way in the future, tend to slot more narrowly into predictable categories; that is part of their identity. Homogeneous churches grow faster and look stronger. But they impoverish themselves and those from whom they divide, and they do nothing to reflect the astounding catholicity of the New Testament. The richness of many an inner-city parish lies in its ever-changing variety; happy is the church that reflects such wealth in its membership.

Parables

Spurgeon's parable of the established church was that of the rotten tree. John Wesley likened her faults rather to the sooty grime on the face of Westminster Abbey—not to mention the monuments inside! But another image flows past our parish as its southern boundary; London's river itself, curving round from Wapping and Shadwell into Limehouse Reach. then on towards Greenwich and the sea. It had once reached a state of advanced pollution. In more than one novel, Charles Dickens describes it so, and the trade in the bodies of the drowned which went on within yards of Limehouse Causeway. But now, you may catch fish here again! So the church also flows on; sometimes the pollution is almost suffocating, but while there is hope of purification we can hardly dig another river, or pretend that Father Thames does not exist at all.

In the end, however, such models prove nothing; like the extended analogy in Swift's 'Tale of a Tub', they are illustrations rather than arguments. They cannot survive apart from solid facts, nor by themselves convince the unpersuaded. So I have set down some local facts as I see them; there remains one final point.

God forbid that I should say 'The C. of E. is best; that is why I am in it.' The reasons for one's own membership have to do with numberless other factors from childhood onwards; sometimes I am hardly persuaded that she is 'the best'— whatever that may mean. We can trap ourselves too easily into producing doctrinal or pragmatic arguments for an Anglican position, while knowing in our hearts that it does not always work in the way we have set it down. Some of my own pictures are exaggerated caricatures; some are true for only part of the time, and in only some of the places.

But being Anglican includes a measure of depressiveness. When our failings are highlighted by those outside our ranks, we want to say 'Is that all that worries you? My word, we have sins you have never dreamed of!' Among the worst may be our tragic faith in our own strength and importance and glory. But where we are most proud, there we are also most weak and pitiable. What is all this pomp and power, this ceremony and influence, this fawning upon royalty, government, business, or the media? How we love it; and how it can squeeze the very life out of us!

So we strut and prance for public acclaim; we gaze in the mirror, grasp at headlines, parade our status—and do not see how vulnerably, miserably poor we make ourselves. We are not alone; but with us the complaint is chronic. If the Bible has not yet taught us where love of the world leads, and what trust in mammon produces, we are novices still. Thank God it may; pray God it will!

But the answer to triumphalism is not defeatism; neither complacency nor despair can be allowed any victories. My claim is not to be staying, in my wisdom, with a Christian communion that is better than the rest; if it were so superior, what would I be doing in it? I count it an amazing joy to belong to such a muddled and maddening body, because it still has room for people like me, and for the love and the kingdom and the good news of God.

Above all in the cities of contemporary Britain, the Church of England is far too good to write off, far too useful to ignore, and far too bad to desert.

6

NOT FORGETTING RURAL ENGLAND

by

*John Richardson**

From the heart of rural England

It is a lovely Autumn afternoon. The sun is beating in through the windows. My hostess has given me a good lunch—home-made soup, scrumptious roast beef salad and her own version of local apple crumble. Cheese and biscuits follow with coffee. Here I am in the heart of rural England, in a small village in the South-West surrounded by the love and care of Christian people, with the sound of cattle lowing, the smell of the farm-yard amidst the activity on the land.

There is a knock on the door. It is the local vicar. He has been looking after three churches for some fourteen years. His visiting, pastoral care and teaching is appreciated by the Christians in the village. But it is hard work, and moves are now being made by him and his parish to hold a Celebration of Faith. The three parishes are preparing as one parish for their mission. Members of the congregation are asked to spend time each day praying for God's guidance for their venture together.

Two days ago a small team of some dozen people were

---

*John Richardson is vicar of a developing new town centre parish in Nailsea, Avon. He is Bishop's advisor in evangelism in the rural Diocese of Bath and Wells having previously been incumbent of four rural parishes and Assistant Missioner in the Diocese of Salisbury. Sue, his wife, comes from a farming and rural background and they have three children. He is a founding member of the Federation of Rural Evangelism and is chaplain to the Royal Bath and West Show.

meeting in a small village hall serving three village communities. It was the last week-end of a ten-day rural mission. Over 50% of the residents had been to evangelistic house meetings and all the homes and residents of the villages had been visited. Forty people were counselled and prayed with at mission events for various reasons, but many made first-time commitments to Christ. The mission planned and executed over two years had come to stay.

It is hard work. It is a slow business. But God is at work in the heart of rural England.

Three months ago a rural Norman market town with an impressive history had its first-ever parish mission. The vicar and his church council had been preparing and planning it for two years. This small group of some dozen people had prayed earnestly and worked hard to come alongside their friends and neighbours. A ten-day mission took place centred on church services, community activities, school out-of-hours clubs and in homes. A men's supper in a local hostelry attracted seventy men, the majority of whom had no concept of Christianity. During that time many were helped in their discipleship. These folk are now being followed up in nurture groups, and are being integrated, step-by-step, into church life. They are being used by the Holy Spirit in their everyday life at home and at work. Such is the hope and encouragement for evangelism and renewal in rural England. Where the Spirit of God is at work among God's people, there is hope and life in the community.

Three completely different situations. There are thousands more.

In 1920, a couple took over the running of their uncle's farm in rural Dorset. They were in their early twenties and newly married. The wife had found a personal faith in the living Christ at the local beach mission some years earlier while on holiday. Her Christian parents nurtured the faith of the family on Bible readings and prayers each day after breakfast and supper. Her husband, too, came from a Christian home in a seaside town where there had been a Bible preaching ministry. As newly-weds, recently arrived in the village, they began to live their lives for Christ as husband and wife, as father and mother, as employer and landlord. Daily Bible reading and prayer in the home, attendance at the local church, witness in the local community among the thirteen homes of the hamlet was the order of the day for sixty years until 1980. There were regularly six to ten people in church every Sunday during those years.

On the other side of the railway line, there is another Christian family whose roots go back some 600 years. They too had Christians in every generation of the family and a private chapel in the house, where the family and its employees would gather at the beginning of each day. Daily worship, daily witness and daily work were the foundations of life in that hamlet. They had also worshipped with the other farmer and his wife until 1980. One sows and another reaps.

In 1980 a new vicar arrived, to work alongside the sixty occupiers of the homes in the two hamlets. Within three weeks all had been visited and friendships were growing. Within twelve months a Sunday School had been started, to which all the thirteen children of the village came fortnight by fortnight. Some of their parents started to attend church. Six people—the eldest 85, the youngest 63—joined the vicar and his wife on Wednesday evenings in the Vicarage for Bible study, discussion and prayer. Within two years there were regularly forty adults and children worshipping in that church. The churchwardens reported in the log book:

> In the last eighteen months revival has hit this community. God has become real to so many, our prayers are being answered and our faith is being strengthened. It is lovely to be part of God's renewal at the ages of 85 and 73.

The secret of all this slipped out on that vicar's farewell evening. For many years the two churchwardens and their wives had met every Sunday evening, apart from holidays. They had prayed for the people of the villages by name, as individuals and as families. The Bible was read and discussed and lived out step-by-step, and after sixty years of earnest and faithful ministry God blew his Spirit upon those villages. That work continues today among those same people. Such is the hope for the rural backwaters of England.

The hallmarks of the kingdom of God

In rural England, like anywhere else, Christians within the Church of England are in business for the Kingdom of God. Christ is changing lives by the score, in gradual, slow but definite ways. Faithfulness, prayer and perseverance based upon hard work and slog are helping rural Christians to find hope. Shared ministry, with clergy and laity working together, is a sign that all is not lost in the countryside. Most are considering the pattern and model of Jesus' ministry. Gone are the days when the vicar can do it all himself. The days are here when ministry together is the task of the whole people of God—yes, even in the heart of rural England. These are encouraging signs, if we would only stop and listen.

The cycle of the seasons

The seasons of the year have much to teach us about rural ministry. Growth and harvest are long, slow processes. When ministering in such places over the past few years I have been amazed at the confidence that some Christians have in speaking of their faith in Jesus. The fears of others are being dealt with as they face the reality of an eternity without Christ. What some have faithfully sown, others have reluctantly reaped. Holiness, the power of prayer, the endurance of faithful ministry by clergy and laity alike have, over the years, brought the Kingdom of God to much of the countryside.

The long winter of apparent deadness reminds the rural dweller of the deep energy and resources of the soil. During the winter months the trees and plants conserve and build up their energy ready for the rapid burst of the early Spring. Buds appear and leaves break forth as the new life of Spring moves rapidly on. Soon comes the first-fruits of Summer and then growth to maturity before the harvest when 'all is safely gathered in'. This process continues year in and year out.

'While the earth remains, seedtime and harvest shall not fail.'
What a future! What an insight into the hope that rural
ministry in England gives us! This is the other side—the
expectancy that God is at work in the countryside—rather
than a constant pre-occupation with the problems of a declining rural church. Indeed Jesus himself understood the cycle of
the seasons, as he taught by parables from the rural scene.

The changing rural communities

As the small rural communities of our country are served,
and we work in them for Christ and his people, there needs to
be an awareness that interests and approaches change with
the movement of time. The 'rural community' (whatever that
is) is changing fast, and the community is becoming home-
centred. The small village church needs servicing effectively
and efficiently. Worship, prayer groups, church planting,
house groups, and church growth are important and critical
areas for discussion and development, remembering all the
advantages of small groups.

Evangelism through the small church in the countryside
needs careful consideration as the expectations of rural
evangelism are worked out. The people and the possibilities
should be considered. Deaneries working together in mission
and evangelism; faith-sharing teams; outreach to young
people; Christians retiring to the countryside; opportunities
for evangelism through local radio and at the local shows and
events—these are all traditional ways which can be used
effectively for Christ.

People and possibilities

So we come to the point where we see that the rural church is
not as 'monochrome' or 'anonymous' as, say, the suburban or
town or inner city scene. There is variety in rural ministry and
evangelism. In rural society we find some of the following
strands: there are villagers of all ages and backgrounds, there
are retired people, some of whom are community-minded
and others who react against, and positively resist, change.

There are those with 'the roses around the cottage door' mentality—the rural village is their idea of heaven and no one will spoil it for them. There are farm workers and their families; land-owners, tenant farmers, owners and employers. Some villages are seeing an influx of professional people like solicitors, doctors, executives, Her Majesty's Forces personnel and civil servants. Other villages have facilities for one-parent families. Others attract people with social problems, gipsies, peace campaigners, travellers and those looking for the alternative society. There are those who live in rented accommodation, caravanners, campers, visitors, holiday-makers, tourists, week-enders and those with second homes. In addition there are elderly folk in residential homes, warden-controlled sheltered accommodation and almshouses.

The situation within any village community is quite complex but full of opportunity. People are people; and as Christians come alongside and listen there are many openings for sharing the good news of Christ by building trust and confidence.

The overall situation

To enable growth and a future for the church in rural England, honesty and realism are needed about the overall situation of each place. An overall vision with long-term goals and short-term objectives must be coupled with the necessary tools of training and continuing education of all Christians in the situation. There needs to be a rediscovery of the meaning and potential of relationships. Perhaps a revival of the cottage meeting or house meeting would help, as some places where parish missions have recently taken place have shown. Rural communities are remarkably homely and friendly, once folk are established and accepted. Such foundations need to be built upon.

The nature of the rural church

There must be a further realization of the nature of the church. It is not limited to the place or situation, but is built upon the experience of the people there who make up the congregation of the body of Christ. This gives hope because the living God is at work in the whole of his church, wherever that is worked out in practice in the local community.

We must care for rural England. There is hope—there is faith—there is opportunity—but it is not easy, as many who have worked in rural ministry for decades will testify.

There are thirteen million people living in rural Britain and occupying 90% of the total land area. Most of these are unevangelized. In a village everybody has an expectation about the nature of the local church and the role of the parson. This is the Church of England's opportunity—positive, heartening and encouraging.

The time has come for the Christian in the countryside to take heed to himself, to his doctrine, to his family and to his flock. The greatest tool to meet this opportunity is the quality of personal holiness which will show itself in the quality and compassion of friendship and relationships. There must be an openness to God, because people matter for the sake of Jesus. The rural Christians are called to be a warm people, taking a message of love to an often cold and alienated community.

Rural Anglicanism

In Britain today there are three and three-quarter million juveniles under the age of 14 living in rural areas. Leslie Francis in his controversial book *Rural Anglicanism* states clearly that the main strength of the Church of England is still in the countryside. He states from his research that in a typical rural diocese this means that only 3.8% of the population go to church on Sunday, only 7.3% register themselves on the electoral roll of parishes, and only 36% of infants are baptized. He shows how the decline in rural Anglicanism has occurred over the past thirty years. He points out from two detailed surveys in one diocese the major strengths and weaknesses of the rural church. In particular he emphasizes the central place of children and young people—both as an essential part of the life of the church today and as an important indication of the future for the church of tomorrow. It is a timely and devastating book, which must make those with responsibility for the rural church reflect and think and act. The questions he asks are worthy of discussion by any rural church's Parochial Church Council.

We can criticize the report until we are blue in the face, but its message must be noted; though we can challenge the basic assumption, which is perhaps suburban, that a measure of the health of a church is whether it can support and sustain an active youth fellowship. In rural communities where families are close, youth fellowships are not the measure of the church's virility. The acid test is the ability of the church to be an effective pastoral agency through the whole of one's life. My experience was that young people were lost shortly after confirmation; and they returned when they got married and started their own families, normally at the point of baptism or attendance at Sunday School.

In responding to *Rural Anglicanism*, though, we must consider the 300,000 farming communities and the 45,000 isolated hill farms not touched by mainstream Christianity. As an established church we must care about the thousands of village churches that have been closed in recent years and the many more that are faced with closure due to diminishing elderly congregations and the need for pastoral leadership. We must also mention the closure of many Methodist chapels and Baptist churches.

Country towns, villages and hamlets outside the influence of mainstream evangelism and the scores of rural communities that are void of ministry to children and young people must have resources of manpower and money poured into them by those in authority. Vision and not survival, growth and not decline, hope and not defeat, prayer and not complacency must be the concern and compassion of the wider church. These are the seeds of hope. Care must be given to ministers, who, because of pastoral duties to several scattered country parishes, are under considerable pressure. They must be helped to accept, train and work with able, committed, sensitive Christian lay leadership from within the local church. Suspicion must be replaced by trust, fear by confidence, reluctance by delegation; as together they move forward, sharing the ministry of all God's gifts in the local church and community.

Church growth

> If the preservation of its church buildings is an indication of the strength of Rural Anglicanism, the Church of England seems to be maintaining its position very well, especially when comparison is made with the . . . decline of the rural Free Churches.[1]

But what kind of spirituality does this offer the rural community, as rural Anglicanism proclaims the gospel of Christ in an increasingly difficult market place? Clearly cultural, educational and social change is rapidly occurring, economics and inflation are hitting hard, decline of vocations and lack of manpower and resources are hindering the proclamation.

In responding to this situation church growth must be the main priority, whereby the local church and individuals come face to face with the realities of personal faith in Jesus Christ, of biblical thinking and of realistic action.

Worship, witness and work among young Christians is the key.

The priorities

> The time is right for the rural Anglican church to re-evaluate its priorities and to re-design its strategies if it is to make a significant impact . . . during the last part of the 20th century.[2]

The task of the local church is to understand what it has to offer in terms of the good news of Jesus Christ—stated in belief and lived out in practice. Local Christians will have to listen to the questions and needs of the local community as it faces up to the challenge of the good news of Jesus Christ. This means we come alongside, listen, understand, share testimonies, stories and personal encounters of Christ, elicit responses, provide nurture and follow-up, and plan growth to maturity. These are the signs of hope in rural England.

The strategy

In considering a strategy for rural Anglicanism, we are being invited to a mission of prayer, action, commitment and thanksgiving. This is based on a definite training programme: preparing the sharers (the rural Christians), locating the seekers (the rural people) and bringing sharers and seekers together on common ground to discuss, question and live out the difference between apostolic Christianity and folk religion.

> Real hope for the future comes when there is vision given the strategy, the faith and the resources.[3]

The challenge

> The countryside is now as much a pastoral challenge to today's church as the inner city. How does Rural Anglicanism successfully proclaim the Gospel of Christ and what kind of spirituality is the church able to offer those communities it was once designed to serve?[4]

Personal holiness is our greatest tool as we plan strategically. Prepare well, and give as Jesus gives to make it all come true. This is at the heart of the effective use of manpower and resources as pastoral and evangelistic strategies are aimed at the rural people. This is the challenge to evangelism and renewal; in the preparation we need, the message we proclaim, the ministry we share, the challenge we present and the strategies we adopt. So we move forward one step at a time, orthodox in faith and radical in practice.

Ministry of the laity

The ministry of the laity is crucial to any hope we have for rural England. The style of lay ministry will vary considerably from one village to another depending on size, compactness, situations, facilities and personnel. There are endless opportunities, including informal 'street warden' schemes where any situation from scattered hamlets to 'service villages' organize and administer caring groups for those in need. In some dioceses, deaneries and parishes, lay people have been licensed to take services of worship in their local churches each Sunday. The encouragement of magazine, community newspaper and parish newsletter distributors is a vital role, because they visit many homes every month. Friendships develop month by month, as trust and confidence between people grows. As one village Christian recently told me: 'It is the monthly Chinese water torture method which has impact in the long term—a steady, constant drip!'

In many situations leaders and helpers are being trained in local centres, for children's and young people's groups, women's groups, prayer groups, Bible study and discussion groups, Lent and Advent courses and Holiday clubs. Most of this training needs to be 'on the job', using resources from neighbouring churches, from the deaneries, from the dioceses and from the specialist rural organizations such as the Federation for Rural Evangelism, The Arthur Rank Centre Stoneleigh, The Rural Theology Association, The Church Army, and Mission for Christ—Rural Evangelism.

In the country the use of the sympathetic fringe people of the rural community as well as practising Christians is vitally important, hoping and praying that both groups will work together growing in faith and trust of God. These limitations must be recognized; movements forward for God come one step at a time. We come alongside people building friendships, listening to the deep questions about life and death and sharing our own personal encounter of God. When the time is ready, such enquirers are helped to make a personal response to Jesus Christ before being nurtured and built up and integrated into the everyday worship, work and witness of the local church in the village.

The oblique evangelism

In a situation where a church is very much part of the community, it is sometimes hard to mix 'evangelism' and the 'countryside' although there are often many opportunities for oblique evangelism during the course of the year's events.

Each has great potential. For example: baptisms, weddings, funerals, community events and the major festivals provide occasions when people turn out in force and often pack the village church. In all this we need to ask the question: 'What are we asking people to become?' In rural evangelism the question will be answered in differing ways because no two contexts are the same. However, the hope is that people are people with needs of acceptance, love, wholeness, value and salvation. Therefore in answering such a question we must take seriously an answer which at its foundations says our aim is to know Christ personally, to think biblically and to act realistically. This is at the heart of apostolic Christianity, for which so many Christians are working faithfully and lovingly against all the claims of implicit and folk religion.

Future hope

The hope for the Church of England in the next few years is that Christians will build on the blended roots of the past working out plans and strategies for worship, ministry, evangelism and care within the community against the social background of the situation. This will mean an analysing of the situation, recognizing allies and moving forward not as a 'holy huddle' but as a body building up the Christian faith from all sections, ages, backgrounds and cultures. Rural Christians will need to ask: What is the worth of our local church? What is the nature of our local community? Where do the church and community work together? In the light of such questions and discussions, rural Christians are beginning to see what their priorities are with short- and long-term perspectives.

Such discussions within the reality of the body of Christ will open up new visions and understandings of the heart of God's love in Christ working in and with the power of his Spirit. Lives are, and will be, changed. Communities are, and will be, transformed. The days in rural England are as exciting and challenging as ever they were. Opportunities for living out the Christian life in practice are endless, provided

Christians move on in faith and hope.

The smaller the situation, the more encouraging evange-listic outreach can be. The possibility of using homes in some villages is helping to stimulate and encourage small groups of Christians. Where relationships between the minister and the laity are good, then shared ministry is blossoming as steps of faith are made, based on the foundations of prayer as communities are influenced by the love of Christ. However, it is hard work and time-consuming. In some places there is an immediate response as people come to a living faith in Christ. In others there is no measurable success to point to, only the hope that God will take what has been offered and use it for the continuing building of his kingdom in the rural areas.

No easy answers

And so the hope for rural England is there. It is not an easy job, but it is a rewarding one for those with vision, patience, stamina and love as they rely daily on the enabling of God's Spirit. Clearly the priorities of Sunday worship, effective prayer and loving, caring relationships are the secrets as Christians become the main agents of hope—living out the hallmarks of the Christian life in their everyday lives.

Recently twenty people from seventeen separate parishes from a large rural diocese met together. It was their third Saturday that year away from their villages and families. They were together listening, praying, learning and sharing what God is doing in their small villages. All of them spoke with warmth and affection of what God is doing as a result of prayer groups, Bible study, worship in small groups and practical Christian living. They spoke of reconciliation and healing between villages, and how through the breaking down of old family hostilities, prayer had changed grave and impossible situations. . . . We could go on.

Oh yes, there were huge problems as well – old buildings, graveyards, small congregations, overworked clergy, growing interest in the occult and alternative ways of living. But as one contributor said: 'Let's look at where God is working and be encouraged. Let's consider the reasons for moving forward. Let's be confident. Let's be outgoing. Let's press on. For "God and us" is a majority. Let's move forward in faith together, putting first things first.'

Never forget rural England

In rural England there are many rays and signs of hope, such as acceptable worship, love for each other and for the under-privileged, Christian family life, shared leadership and ministry and an openness to God based on the priority of people's real needs against the backcloth of the prophets of doom and resistance to change. The time has come not to opt out but to opt in. God is actively at work in the lives of families, communities and his church. The opportunities are there, the people are there and so are the resources. They need though to be pruned, encouraged, watered, fed, developed, surrounded by love, founded in prayer—for the deserts, the wastelands, the rural areas are places where God is doing new things now—and where God will do new things in the future. Consequently we must not lose hope. We must move on and out, going in peace to love and serve the Lord.

Never forget rural England. For God is always there.

7

GROWING ON THE GROUND

by

*Ian Bunting**

Growing churches are successful churches. A controversial
Bishop of Birmingham, E. W. Barnes, once seemed to
deny it: 'When it comes to religion, nothing fails like success.' He spoke, I guess, out of a deep disillusionment with
Victorian triumphalism and over-confidence about the nature
of the kingdom of God. Regrettably, the Church of England
has adopted his view in a way which can never be justified
from an unbiased interpretation of the New Testament. There
is no shadow of doubt that Jesus and his apostles expected the
kingdom of God to grow and to extend itself to the ends of the
world. They stood in the authentic prophetic tradition; 'My
word . . . will not fail to do what I plan for it; it will do everything I send it to do' (Is 55:11).

When some modern bishops and priests wish to add to the
Litany 'From successful churches, Good Lord deliver us',
they are in danger of confusing two distinct issues: size and
purpose. Maybe they have in mind the suburban congregation
whose different members commute some distance to attend a
congenial form of worship. It is true that such a church can
exist in splendid isolation from its neighbours, and suck the
Christian life out of other areas of the town which would

---

*Ian Bunting served successively as Vicar of St John's, Waterloo, Liverpool
and Director of Pastoral Studies at Cranmer Hall, Durham before being
appointed Rector of Chester-le-Street on the edge of the Tyne and Wear
conurbations. A feature of the ministry at Chester-le-Street has been the
development of six separate congregations apart from the parish church.

benefit enormously from the contribution of capable Christians who desert it for a more favourable climate. What is wrong about such a judgement is that it fails to treat success in terms of the purpose of the church and tends therefore to justify the inward-looking, pre-occupied and unadventurous congregation. The large church, certainly, may be failing to proclaim the conquering word of God. The small, struggling congregation may be doing it marvellously. The point I am making is that successful Christian growth can happen in large and small congregations. Successful churches are growing churches, where the kingdom of God is growing through the life and witness of the members.

The purpose of the church

The standard by which we judge success or failure is not therefore in terms of size or activity but of purpose. The purpose of the church is identical with that set before the disciples by Jesus, and modelled in his own ministry. He came to introduce the kingdom of God, to choose his personal agents and to multiply the number of those who would bear witness to it. The Church of England, as we shall see, is still well placed to fulfil Jesus' mission. But first we shall spell out the purpose of the church and the sort of growth we may expect to see when it is successfully accomplishing its purpose.

1. *We shall see the church growing together in love.* Mutual love is both evidence for, and the consequence of, the life of the body of Christ. In Ephesians 4:15–16 we see how the apostle speaks of a spiritual maturity which shows itself as each separate part works harmoniously both with Christ and with each other. The local church has, as its most powerful growing medium, a Christ-controlled style of life together.

2. *We shall see the church growing in spiritual and moral uprightness.* Immature Christians, who are content to stand still in their development, do nothing to extend God's kingdom in themselves or in anyone else. In 1 Peter 2:1–2, the apostle looks for an increase in moral stature and spiritual

hunger. Such a goal calls the local church to a serious engagement with the task of enabling believers to learn their faith and to grow in grace.

3. *We shall see the church growing in love and service to the world God loves.* In Galatians 6:9–10, the apostle tells of a forthcoming and eternal harvest for those who go on doing good both inside and outside the household of faith. There will be a lack of discrimination about a ministry which matches that of Jesus. It includes all and excludes none. They are certainly right who criticize those churches which succeed only at the expense of others and which, while enjoying a rich intimate life on their own, disregard the crying needs on their doorsteps.

4. *We shall see the church growing in numbers.* I have left this point until last because it is the way people have commonly judged success. I want to say that it is a necessary goal but not a sure mark of success. In the Gospels, Jesus told many parables of growth and commissioned his followers to make more disciples. It is the unmistakable mission of the church to increase the number of effective signs and witnesses to God's kingdom (Mt 28:19). The churches have never been true to their calling when they have sat back and waited for people to respond to their message. There is an inescapable element of claim in the gospel, and churches have the responsibility of bringing it to the ears of all.

The mission of the Church of England

How, then, is the Church of England so well-placed to fulfil the mission of Jesus today? Because she is there. Anglicans often hold on by their fingertips but, even in urban priority areas and in scattered rural communities, they still maintain a Christian presence and witness. For this reason, it is sad to see the Church of England suffering from withdrawal symptoms. We are in retreat from the feeling of responsibility, which we used readily to accept, for all who live in our parishes. We have been moving inexorably from a communal to an associational model, from church to sect. This is because we will insist on thinking of the church in terms of its members rather than its purpose. The condition is not helped by an over-emphasis today upon sacramental worship. Sacramental worship, demanding at present the presence of male ordained priests, leads to the situation where over-loaded clergy hasten around small congregations meeting at odd hours and in inaccessible places. It does not foster missionary passion in priest or people.

The commitment of the Church of England to the parochial system is one foundation for a commitment to mission. For a generation prophets of doom have been foretelling its collapse, because of the burden of maintaining decaying buildings on the one hand and the decline in the number of clergy on the other. Whatever made us think that the survival of the church depended on bricks and mortar or professional Christians? The New Testament Church grew and prospered without either advantage; or is it a handicap? What those believers could not do without was apostles and elders. The apostles planted churches and appointed elders—in the plural—to lead them. They established a corporate witness to Christ as the Christians in a community gathered to worship and to express their new life in Christ. They left behind authorized office-holders to maintain the structured congregations and to equip the people for their own Christian ministry (Eph 4:12). Anglicans have stepped into that tradition.

Time for planting

In the Old Testament the preacher reminds us that God chooses 'the time for planting and the time for pulling up' (Eccles 3:2). The New Testament encourages us to believe that we live in the age of the Holy Spirit, and that it is the day for planting and not for pulling up. In 1 Corinthians 3:7–9 St Paul describes himself and his fellow evangelists as partners working in God's field, sowing and watering, in the knowledge that God will bring the growth.

A hundred years ago the Church of England recognized and accepted this vocation. Even if we lagged far behind the

Methodists in our efforts, we brought the ministry of the church to the people in the communities where they lived.

My predecessor, Canon W. O. Blunt, Rector of Chester-le-Street a hundred years ago, determined 'that the outlying parts of the parish might be provided with means of grace in connection with the Church of England'. This expansionist phase of our history passed, with the years, as the condition of mission churches worsened and the number of assistant curates was depleted.

In our parish alone, in the last twenty years, our three mission churches have been flattened. Let us call spades spades, and acknowledge that we are in retreat. To return to the offensive, we shall need to plant new congregations and equip them with ministers to pastor them. Patrick Blair set this process off in our own town; now we have seven area congregations served by forty-one 'ministers', lay and ordained, who share the leading of the worship and the preaching.

The burgeoning house group movement encourages us to believe that this strategy is possible. During the last twenty years we have seen house groups forming, failing and re-forming for all sorts of purposes. Good house groups, however, display four characteristics which reflect the purpose of the church which we have outlined above.

First, *the house group provides a fellowship,* which is important if Christians are to grow in mutual care and inter-dependence. In the house group, the Christian enjoys a sense of belonging. With the erosion of a strong and extended family life, the small group has brought to lonely and isolated individuals a companionship in the faith which is warm and supportive.

Secondly, *the house group gives Christians the chance to learn, and to grow in the faith.* For centuries, we have become accustomed to a heavily didactic style of Christian education, concentrating on the teacher and what is taught more than on the learner and what is assimilated. Small groups allow for the vital components of clarification, reflection, dialogue, articulation and application to take their place in the process of making mature Christian disciples.

Thirdly, *the house group allows the members to discover, to experiment with and to use their gifts for ministry*. One of the handicaps with which Anglicans have lumbered themselves, perhaps understandably in the light of appalling standards in the mediaeval Church, is the need for a learned ministry. No one would question the need to be learned in the Scriptures but, as most theological teachers and students will know, modern ministerial training has majored upon books about the faith rather than upon the source itself and upon what God is saying in the world and in the church today. The good small group is a great leveller where it is able to affirm all the members, and not just the highly educated, in their particular insights and gifts. Men and women who have been de-skilled by the traditional expectations associated with Anglican ministry, now discover they have something to give to each other within the body of Christ.

Fourthly, *the effective house group pursues an objective beyond its own survival and growth*. Only in so far as it upholds this sense of mission is it likely to avoid the dangers of introversion and to thrive. We have already noted the way in which the Church of England, fascinated with its own problems of survival, has become insular and inward-looking. The good group will look beyond itself. Mission, of course, includes both evangelism and practical care. Nevertheless, in one way or another, or in more than one way, the small group which reaches beyond itself brings life to others and gives light to the world—as we pray in the post-communion prayer of Rite A in the *Alternative Service Book*.

I have started by underlining the value of house groups because a strategy incorporating them is possible in almost any Anglican parish without causing offence to others, even where they attract members of other denominations or meet beyond immediate parochial boundaries. They provide a local Christian presence and witness in the community and, at the same time, as we shall see below, they throw up, in embryo at least, an indigenous ministry.

Alternative churches

In his hard-hitting book, *The Church of England: Where is it going?* (Kingsway, 1985), David Holloway asks us to consider the possibility of setting up what he calls 'alternative churches'. This very provocative idea immediately makes the hackles of the parochial clergy rise in alarm. It seems to run counter to all the traditional tenets of English Anglicanism. The vicar is pope in his parish and woe betide the colleague who steps over the boundaries to exercise any ministry without permission. Such parochialism stifles evangelistic initiatives; one hopes that it will die slowly as clergy learn to recognize their neighbours as brothers rather than as competitors. Let me say at the outset, however, that I believe it is possible to plant alternative churches within many parishes and, with the co-operation of others, in nearby parishes as well. The first is happening already, the second will happen where we are able to shed at least a little of our stubborn defensiveness.

It seems to me entirely appropriate to envisage the opening of such alternative churches in parts of the parish which other services do not reach. Probably they will be more than house churches. The congregation will gather in any convenient, and sometimes not convenient, building which is available for the purpose. Schools are particularly suitable for family services because parents and children are usually happy in the links which such buildings have with the community they serve. The same is true of village halls and community centres. Pubs and clubs, while not ideal for families and children, often provide a very attractive venue for men to meet in. The important factor is the nature of the community the alternative church is aiming to serve. It is a much more complicated business than it may at first appear. For instance, it is not simply a question of scattering congregations around the area. There are geographical and socio-economic, cultural and psychological considerations to take into account.

In our parish two area congregations meet within a few hundred yards of each other. One serves a predominantly owner-occupied estate full of young families. The other attracts the residents of a huge council estate. The style of church life differs too, each reflecting the cultural context in which it is set. What is the advantage of this arrangement? Each congregation has thrown up its own leaders and adopted its own style of fellowship and service. Contrary to what one might expect, they have not only increased the number of worshippers, they have also served to build up a common allegiance to the parish church. True, some have never yet crossed its threshold, but others have taken up responsibilities which tether them to the life of the whole congregation in a way which was foreign to them before these semi-autonomous, dispersed congregations were formed. In the context of growing churches and disciples, the strategy has proved successful.

The parochial system, by which we all live within the geographical boundary of an Anglican parish, for which a priest and congregation are responsible, creates the possibility of points of contact; and not only at the critical pastoral moments of birth, marriage and death. Priest and people still capitalize upon the opportunities, old and new, which the system affords. The problem arises when we need to break out of parochial constraints or to cross over parochial boundaries in order to promote the kind of growth of which we have been speaking. We cannot do it without creating the suspicion that we are trespassing or being critical of Christians in other places, in different circumstances and, possibly, with divergent gifts.

United we fall

One of the most depressing features of the church in the United Kingdom is the way most Christians enthuse about Christian unity and miserably fail to achieve progress in uniting the churches. We are told that unity is something the Spirit gives (Eph 4:3), so perhaps the sad tale of our fruitless efforts should not surprise us. Nevertheless there has been a notable and positive shift in the character of ecumenical activity. Most of us now try to spotlight the points of unity rather than the points of division. This has led to a greater willingness to recognize my erstwhile enemy as a brother, a fellow-Christian who is therefore engaged in the same mission as I am. I relish the memory of the recent joint churches' Youth Festival where Roman Catholics and Pentecostalists, from our town, served side-by-side in an evangelistic coffee bar which featured addresses by a Roman Catholic priest and a Pentecostalist evangelist. With so many divergencies within Anglicanism most of us are able to recognize that these differences need not for ever inhibit joint initiatives in the cause of Christ. We may squabble like ducks in a duck-pond but all Anglicans are committed, together with their ordained priests, 'to make Christ known to all men'. We fulfil this in a number of different ways; by the evangelistic thrust of our baptisms, weddings and funerals, by our position as the church of the land and by an increasing, if sometimes theoretical, willingness to co-operate with all Christians in the work of mission. This longer vision, much bigger than the concerns of any one church or nation, helps us to keep the Church of England and its members in the front line. The small group, and the larger 'alternative church' can become very cosy and contented if the light of battle dims in the eye. No Anglican, however, should be able to settle for a comfortable life in the barracks. He is part of a nationwide offensive, a global campaign. The enormous scale of the task calls for the united effort of all Christian believers no matter what their differences. Yet here we come up against the major obstacle.

The Church of England has never been able to develop effective structures for evangelism. The parochial system has admirably suited a pastoral ministry to men and women who call themselves Christians and identify with the local church. When it comes to breaking new ground we need a greater flexibility in worship; for example, a more aggressive style of ministry and—I have already suggested—a renewed understanding of the purpose of the church. I began by saying that the successful church was the growing church. Many Anglicans, and others, have turned up their noses at the idea because they think we are talking about numbers when, they say, we ought to be talking about faithfulness. Perhaps they have in mind the little town or country parish where a godly priest says his prayers and ministers conscientiously to the congregation which comprises all who have not consciously opted out of the fold by joining some other denomination. That is what God wants, they say; a little group of faithful worshippers leavening the whole parish by their love, prayers and worship. A hundred years ago that strategy seemed to work. It had appeared to work for the previous millennium. Nevertheless forces were operating in Western civilization which were threatening this idea of the church and the community. We talk frequently about the secularizing effect of the 18th century Enlightenment, but it was more than that. The church was being marginalized.

In our own parish two significant changes took place at the beginning of this century, to be followed later by others. In the first place the Church of England was losing her influence in the sphere of education. Having pioneered the schooling of our town's children, the church began to lose its grip as non-conformists and others pushed for secular state education. Rightly or wrongly, this effectively reduced the status, position and influence of the church in the community. Even church people began to send their children to state schools as church schools struggled to survive. It could not be long before the ties of the town with the local church began to loosen, and they did. Today, a hundred years after the time when the church controlled the education of the children in our town, we have only a token investment remaining.

In the second place, and in a way more serious, two world wars and the loss of the British Empire led to a cataclysmic loss of confidence in the church's previously confident, perhaps over-confident, affirmations about the nature of the kingdom of God. The optimism of the last century totally evaporated. People no longer believed that the kingdom of God was waiting around the corner. The chill wind rose to gale force here as elsewhere. And, as recent church reports suggest, even rural congregations suffered the same, if delayed, decline.

In the light of these changed circumstances it is totally unrealistic to imagine that old parochial and pastoral expectations are adequate for a whole range of new circumstances.

Colonies of the kingdom

Recently the Bishop of Durham, David Jenkins, has been challenging us to become effective signs of the kingdom of God in the North-East or, as he puts it, 'lively colonies of the kingdom'. He has brought a call to us to turn outwards. But if we are to do that we must take risks, try experiments and cross boundaries. Non-denominational and para-church groups have always been braver in this kind of initiative. Having taken the plunge they get on with the job where our Anglican efforts easily founder upon the rock of diocesan boards and committees. For example, the Diocesan Missioner becomes a useful officer of the Bishop in the areas of ecumenism, spirituality, inter-faith dialogue and evangelism; and yet, all the time, he is merely keeping the same old wheels grinding slowly. Somehow we need to help Christians to look in new directions. I believe this calls for five activities on our part, none of them easy and all of them costly.

First, *we need to think*. It is always much easier, I find, to do things than to think about what we do and the consequence of it. It demands a concentration of mind from which we easily shy away. Nevertheless it is only by thinking through what we believe about God, the world and his church that we can test the validity of any ideas about breaking new ground for God. If government by committee rings the death knell of new initiatives, the 'ideas man' and the 'think-tank' do have an important part to play in thrashing out policies which will extend the church's witness to the kingdom of God. Churches have been developing all sorts of leadership teams. In our case, the Consultative Group, as we call it, has helped us both to avoid making some big mistakes and also to take new directions. There will be no growth without thinking through our objectives and identifying the targets we believe God intends us to achieve.

Secondly, *we need to make adventurous appointments, lay and ordained,* within our congregations. The church has always been inclined to appoint 'safe' men and women. Yet no new ground will be captured without risk and danger. One of the marks of a good appointment in the church is the discomfort caused as the new appointee begins to make the rest of us aware of his vision and calls upon us to support him in his work. I told our recently appointed youth workers that you can often judge the usefulness of a new worker by his nuisance value. They have abundantly lived up to my expectations. Someone has said that the New Testament does not lead us to suppose that nothing should be done for the first time. Our fathers were always reaching out for God and his kingdom. We need to remind ourselves that Christians are often ready to recognize and to support such ventures, and we may call upon them to do so.

Thirdly, *we need to multiply the number of ambassadors, agents or ministers within our congregations.* We frequently find it impossible to move positively because of the weight of existing responsibilities in maintaining the structures. The load will ease when the burden is shared. We will see the way ahead more clearly when we have time and resources to seize our opportunities. As I have said above, this policy calls for the training and equipping of a new indigenous ministry. Local churches are beginning to do this, often with the bishop's approval and blessing. Non-stipendiary priests, preachers, pastors, lay ministers and leadership groups all have a part to play in the growth of the church.

Fourthly, and most painfully, *growing churches will need to release resources to help other churches grow.* Once again, to avoid misunderstanding, I am not simply talking about churches which are growing numerically. Indeed we need to resist the school of thought which argues that the way to grow is to make churches with large memberships grow even larger. Instead, we need growing churches, in the proper sense, to divide in order to multiply. We could do this in a number of ways. The astonishing numerical growth of Pentecostalism in

South America took place because churches divided and then multiplied. Even if the cause of the division was usually disagreement, growth followed. Here in England, we could at least send Christians, in groups, to other parishes or receive them with our blessing instead of with our reluctance or implaccable opposition. Again, we could send workers, or even commission them, to go and work in another part of the town or community. We would only be encouraging what usually happens anyway. The strong eclectic church has an impressive impact upon young and growing Christians in their early years. Sooner or later, however, they find something missing; and out of conviction, or even simply for family reasons, they decide to transfer their allegiance to some nearby and, usually, not nearly so successful church. The sharing of resources becomes an essential ingredient of any recipe to establish lively new colonies of the kingdom of God.

Fifthly, and finally, *we will engage in a constant re-appraisal of our own strategies and ways of working*. The kingdom of God is always on the move and the Holy Spirit is revealing new truths from God's word. Without the benefit of review and re-assessment, churches easily settle into ruts, only to wonder at some stage why the glories and triumphs of the past seem to be unrepeatable as they fade into distant memories. The kingdom of God calls for change, and change is always painful. It is tempting to avoid the pain by refusing to countenance the change, but we do so at the peril of forfeiting the Spirit's guidance and help in implementing what is often costly and distressing. One of our churchwardens, Tommy Heeley, used to make the point with a colourful family illustration: 'If the children of the household are silent, they must be sick!' There is a healthy rumpus and a wholesome disturbance in the family of God which is willing to review its priorities and re-align its goals according to the wisdom of the Holy Spirit.

In this chapter I have tried to trace the hope of the Church of England not in her members, nor in her reputed strengths, but rather in the purpose to which we are called as servants of the kingdom of God. In so far as that purpose reflects the purpose of Jesus Christ, we may look for the same kind of growth he anticipated as he commissioned the disciples to carry forward his own mission. There is certainly, by such criteria, no room for despair.

8

RENEWAL IN THE PARISH CHURCH

by

*Tom Walker**

Over the last quarter of a century many of the main denominations of the worldwide church have been experiencing a
new spiritual movement. It is most generally referred to as
the 'Renewal movement' or the 'Charismatic Renewal'. The
Church of England has been notably touched by this
movement, and in November 1978 the General Synod asked
for a report to be prepared, 'noting the rise in recent years of
the Charismatic movement within the Church of England
and being concerned to conserve the new life it has brought
into many parishes.' The report was to 'explore the reasons
for this upsurge, pinpoint the particular distinctive features
of spirituality and ethos which the movement presents, and
indicate both the points of tension which exist with traditional Anglicanism and also how the riches of the movement
may be conserved for the good of the Church.'

Although it is described as a 'movement', the Renewal is
hardly a defined movement like the Boy Scout movement
with its initiating promise and its Scout laws. Indeed the
Renewal movement is as hard to pin down as the Holy Spirit

---

*Canon Tom Walker has been Vicar of St John's Harborne, Birmingham
since 1970 after serving on the staff of Birmingham Cathedral as Succentor.
He has been chairman of the House of Clergy in the diocese since 1982 and
is a member of General Synod. St John's has an emphasis on praise and
prayer with a full programme of evangelism and training for lay leadership.
Tom frequently takes teams from the church on mission and renewal
weekends.

of God himself. Speaking to Nicodemus Jesus said, 'The wind blows where it wills, and you hear the sound of it, but you do not know whence it comes or whither it goes; so it is with everyone who is born of the Spirit' (Jn 3:8). And so it is with everyone renewed by the Spirit. There is a sovereignty of God's action at the heart of renewal, and although there are evidences of his working in changing people's lives, and also in bringing local churches to a new expression of spiritual life, God's action is hard to pin down. His way of working is as varied as creation itself. He never exactly repeats himself in two people's lives. The characteristics of one renewed church will differ from another, and yet there are common features which show that renewal is taking place. Those involved in renewal talk of a significant step forward in their experience of God the Holy Spirit, accompanied by a deeper discovery of the heavenly Father's love and a new zeal in following Jesus Christ, God's Son. A German youth evangelist, Wolfgang Heiner said: 'It's a pity that Charismatics don't call themselves a "Jesus movement".' In practice that is what it is, for as the Holy Spirit moves afresh in people's lives, he does not draw attention to himself but as Jesus promised: 'He will bear witness to me' (Jn 15:26); 'He will glorify me, for he will take what is mine and declare it to you' (Jn 16:14). So renewed Christians and renewed churches became more Christ-centred.

As a result of this there is a new emphasis on evangelism in order to obey the last command of Jesus: 'Go, therefore, and make disciples of all nations, baptizing them in the name of the Father and of the Son and of the Holy Spirit, teaching them to observe all that I have commanded you; and lo, I am with you always, to the close of the age' (Mt 28:19–20). With the command comes the promise of the presence of Jesus, and a heightened awareness of his power and reality is part of renewal experience. In the congregation of Christians, this leads to a quality of worship previously unknown; and often those churches which have not had a tradition of emphasizing the Eucharist find a new focus on the Lord's Supper as the church's central act of worship.

Christ-centred worship brings a deeper sense of fellowship and unity to God's people, which is discovered as a local church expresses the gifts which the Holy Spirit releases in individual Christians. Instead of one man, the clergyman, ministering in the church, it is suddenly possible, with the insights of the Renewal movement, for every member of the body of Christ to minister to each other. It is truly a church-transforming discovery to find that all have spiritual gifts with which to build up and minister to each other. However, for this to happen, new patterns of corporate worship have to be found, so that in informal meetings as well as in main liturgical services room can be made for these gifts and this ministry to be expressed.

New structures also have to be formed so that the former order of a 'one-man ministry' can be replaced by a corporate ministry involving a number of leaders exercising a shared minority. This is necessary because the renewal of a ministry which leads to rapid growth, successful evangelism, and spiritual ministry to large numbers of people, often stirs up opposition from evil powers. Involvement in spiritual warfare is not something to be undertaken alone. When a string of enquirers seeking deliverance from occult powers arrives for ministry and help, it is vital to have the strength of several people in prayer-fellowship together, to counter the power of evil in Christ's name.

Furthermore, such praying people need the structure of small home groups in which to learn to exercise gifts of ministry and leadership within the larger congregations. Unless Christians are experienced in sharing Jesus with one another and praying for each other on a regular and committed basis, it is asking a great deal to expect that a confident prayer ministry should be given to outsiders. Equally, such home group leaders themselves need pastoral oversight, and many churches have set up a structure of care by means of pastoral elders. In this way the Renewal has led to the corporate expression of gifts from God for ministry to others both within the congregation of believers and outside, and in a far more realistic way the local church has become the body of Christ in its parish.

The question mark that some people have concerning the Renewal is whether this can validly happen within the Church of England. Some feel that the structures are so firmly established, and the pattern of liturgical worship so rigid, that the sort of freedom described above can never be truly experienced in such a traditional setting. As well as rigidity in the local church, there seems to be so much bureaucracy and such a top-heavy hierarchy in the wider church at its central and diocesan levels, that some give up hope of God breathing into such dry bones and freeing such formality. It is partly because there is such little hope for changing the heavy structures of the Church of England that so many turn to the house churches for warmth of fellowship and freedom to express spiritual gifts within the Renewal movement. Indeed the growth of house churches bears witness to a total dissatisfaction with the unrenewed Christianity of mainstream churches. As a recent book by Andrew Walker shows,[5] this new movement, often called the Restoration movement, has developed a pronounced separatist, anti-church quality.

The Restoration groups have often been accused of sheep-stealing, because so much of their growth has come from the previously dissatisfied adherents of other churches. However, in a letter to the *Church of England Newspaper*, Arthur Wallis, a well-known house church leader, denied this charge. He wrote:

Is not this growth (of the house churches) at the expense of other churches? Yes, to a great extent, but that does not make us sheep stealers! It is just that we don't turn away sheep who come looking for green grass and still waters. Do you know any church that does? Thankfully a growing number joining us are new converts with no church connection. We wish they were all like that.

It is because the house churches provide so many of the features of renewal already described that people turn to them for care and succour, deliverance and healing, fellowship and ministry, teaching and security. They challenge traditional, formal, unrenewed churches by their very existence. But sadly there are many signs that all is not well with the teaching and activities of some in the House Church movement. Despite denials, there are many cases of Christians being strongly invited, indeed pressurized, to leave their own church and to join a new house church fellowship.

This actually happened to me at Bradford! Together with Canon David MacInnes, the Birmingham Diocesan Missioner, I was leading a mission at Bradford Cathedral in March 1984. I turned up early one morning at a hotel in the centre of the city where David was speaking at a breakfast meeting for businessmen. At the door I was welcomed by a Christian brother with a warm smile and a firm handshake. Without my clerical collar I might have been any unsuspecting Bradford citizen, though my Southern accent might have suggested that I was immigrant rather than resident. I was quickly approached by another man whom I presumed to be part of the welcome team, and within minutes I was being informed about Harvestime, a leading Bradford house church, and their meetings and activities were being described in glorious terms. I was asked to attend one of their meetings, but by that stage in the conversation I felt I had to come clean and explain that I was in fact one of the Bradford Cathedral missioners!

Others will tell how scriptures are used to persuade them that leaving their own apostate church is vital if they are to become part of God's purpose to restore the purity of the church by establishing Restoration fellowships. There are also many stories of authoritarian eldership being expressed in the house churches, and what is a good provision of God for shared ministry easily becomes distorted into a form of 'shepherding' which interferes with an individual's personal responsibility in decision-making and to some extent destroys human dignity. Those who cannot accept such heavy-handed guidance become casualties who, if rejected by the house church leadership, sometimes find it hard to get back into the church they had previously belonged to, but which they, themselves, had rejected in former days. Such wounded people are left in a no-man's land, and may give up churchgoing altogether with a double disillusionment in their lives.

Although professing a unity and togetherness unknown in mainstream congregations, already the story of the House Church movement is one of split and division, of flux and change. Though it claims to be nondenominational, something very like denominations are becoming established. Some groups are out of fellowship with other groups, and most are not involved greatly with mainline denominations. Whilst I have felt challenged by much of the good teaching and beautifully creative songs which come constantly from this movement, and whilst I long to meet the needs of those who are so manifestly disenchanted with the Church of England and other denominational churches, I am deeply worried; because the tendency of house churches to cream off the cream means inevitably that some will drown in the cream.

I will also prophesy that when the 'pure' Restoration churches have destroyed themselves through leadership rivalry and have dissipated into multitudinous smaller groupings the fuddy-duddy, old-fashioned, parish church will still ring its bells on countless street corners of our land, issuing a free, un-pressurized call to worship. I dare to say that second and third generation youngsters will not grow well on the diet of teaching that tends to characterize 'pure' churches with a programme of hyper-spirituality and with a defensive 'Come out from among them' philosophy and ghetto mentality. Some, I forecast, will then drift back, even to the Church of England.

'Why?' someone asks. Because I believe that the Church of England, within all the muddle of its own historical background and painful Reformation, truly represents the local church of a local place in this country. In the New Testament (as another writer emphasizes), *we do not find Christian communities gathered on particular doctrines, nor centred on notable personalities*. Indeed, in 1 Corinthians

1:12 onwards, Paul deplores such adherence to merely human leadership. In the Corinthian church it led to scandalous division, as different groups within the church said: 'I belong to Paul', or 'I belong to Apollos', or 'I belong to Cephas', or 'I belong to Christ'. In one sense, the value of the Church of England's heavy structure is that there are many safeguards against individuals doing their own thing.

At one point when we had a division of view in our own church at St John's Harborne, we were prevented from splitting apart simply because of the authority of a wise bishop which was expressed in a caring and supportive way. The traditional authority of the bishop was respected. As parish priest I had promised at my ordination to obey the bishop 'in all things lawful and honest', and church members were humble enough to accept his ruling too. We all worked at re-establishing relationships, and in time became the best of friends again. The alternative would have been to have set up rival personalities each with different views and interpretations of what was happening among us, and the congregation could have been invited to follow one or the other. The church would have been split and Satan would have laughed up his (spiritually metaphorical) sleeve. As it was, after some years, we were all able to laugh together at our respective misinterpretations and stupidities.

The same possibility of wise leadership is available to a vicar within the Church of England when renewal first comes to a congregation. It usually comes in the shape of certain enthusiastic individuals who have a testimony about their own personal renewal by the Holy Spirit. Such is the joy of their new discovery of previously unknown spiritual realities and gifts, that they may seem critical of the traditional expression of worship in church, and can often accuse the vicar of not teaching about the fullness of the Spirit from the pulpit. Their views seem often to be proudly expressed and elitist, and though such people desire opportunities to share their new insights, the overwhelmed and criticized vicar is slow to give them leadership, for fear of upsetting others in his flock.

The freedom of ministry is such that a vicar or priest-in-charge is able to absorb the impetus of a group of renewed Christians. He can be part of the group that longs for God to renew the whole church. He can stretch ahead of the keenest renewed person by asking God for spiritual gifts and wisdom to cope with change, advance and growth. He can gently humble the proud by pointing out that if in the early church the evidence of the Spirit's outpouring was to be seen in effective outreach and evangelism, and in a new depth of sharing love (Acts 4:32–35) it was also to be seen in social care of the needy and deprived in the community (Acts 6:1–6). He can point out that the renewing work of the Holy Spirit is to be seen in signs and wonders (Acts 5:12–16) and that the mark of God's grace in the church is not an attitude of criticism and discontentment, but of mutual upbuilding and encouragement (1 Cor 14:3). My own attitude is to press such people forward in busy ministry so that the genuine, eager, spirit-filled Christians find boundless practical opportunities for service while the malcontents are too exhausted to complain! This way, gifts of ministry are discovered and used. The local church is built up and God is seen to move in the wider neighbourhood as well.

The structures of the Church of England are, if not ideal, exceedingly practical for accommodating the change that is inescapable when Renewal comes. The vicar is called to work with his Parochial Church Council in decision-making, but he does not have formally constituted deacons or elders to restrict initiative in the Spirit. His stipend does not depend on pleasing the church members to whom he ministers. The Bishop is hardly likely to restrict ministry in the Spirit which produces growth in outgoing evangelism, social care, and increased giving and love amongst the congregation. In many parishes the existing Standing Committee of the PCC provides an excellent embryo eldership. My predecessor Canon Leathem used the men on his Standing Committee in this way long before I arrived in the parish in Harborne in 1970, long before people even spoke in terms of renewal.

Of course, change needs to be handled with care. Raymond Postgate has said: 'Deploring change is the unchangeable habit of all Englishmen'. But though the church is the arch-conservative institution in our land, at various times of up-heaval and revival, its whole face has changed drastically — not least in recent days with the emphasis in many churches on Parish Communion and with the blossoming of new liturgical forms. Some people criticize the *Alternative Service Book* and its language, but it has broken the rigidity of former time-honoured patterns. Its cadences are briefer, and its flexibility allows for the intrusion of non-liturgical congregational par-ticipation much more readily than the splendid, but heavy Cranmerian prayers. Although those who find security in the old Prayer Book forms often claim Cranmer's inspiration as a defence against new, and some say trite, words in worship, Cranmer himself was a complete radical. He expected absolutely contemporary language and worship and called those not prepared to change 'peevish, perverse and obdurate'.

Some church leaders, unfortunately, insist on change for change's sake. Renewal is not about tinkering with liturgy, or replacing long-loved hymns with worship songs (though many of these are hardly new, since in many cases they are words taken from Scripture). Renewal is about finding our security in the mobility of the Spirit of God and his leading—not in static forms and familiar liturgy. However, the value of retaining traditional forms and liturgical patterns as we have them in the Church of England is that we are not for ever having to stage new climaxes in worship, with ever fresh elements and content to our prayers. Some try to do this. Their motto is 'constant change is here to stay', and it does not work. The sense of awe and wonder in worship is a totally God-given thing, and the joy of Anglican worship is that we can come home to God, slipping into the familiarity of a well-known liturgy, and just relax in God's love as we worship together. Within that relaxation, the creative Spirit-inspired contribution of one and another in the congregation can liven the immediacy of such worship experience and make specific intercessory contributions at the appropriate time in the service.

Inevitably when renewal comes to a church the worship services tend to be longer. There are more elements to be included. Love demands that older hymns are retained for more traditional worshippers. Chanted psalms will be retained for those, like me, who find this a marvellous idiom for wallowing in Scripture—though pointing marks will be provided for all, and from time to time the whole congregation will be introduced into the mystique of chanting psalms and canticles so that it is more and more a corporate, satisfying congregational experience. Prayers will be opened up and sometimes different people will assure each other out loud of God's promises of forgiveness at the time of absolution. Also a renewed congregation becomes more and more hungry for the preaching of God's word, remembering that (in Jim Packer's phrase) 'sermonettes breed Christianettes'. People become dissatisfied with the spiritual equivalent of a diet of MacDonald's chicken dips with variably flavoured sauces. They want preaching that sets forth our Lord Jesus Christ in his victory and majesty and triumph as he has been enthroned for us in the suffering of the cross and exalted by God and given 'the name which is above every name' (Phil 2:9).

As we have in the Church of England a breadth of doctrinal understanding within different groups and parties, some wonder how renewed Gospel-believing Christians can survive in such a church. But the fact is that in its Articles and formularies our church is soaked in Scripture, and the words are just waiting to come alive as they are interpreted in the pulpit and taken home by the Spirit of God. In an article in *The Times* of February 1st 1976, following the publication of the Church of England's Doctrine Commission Report, it was written of the contributors: 'They disagree about almost everything else. An ordinary man in the pew picking up the volume to discover the bedrock beliefs of his church would find that the available options are so wide that anything goes . . . The impression given is that Anglicanism is a religion without doctrine.' Some, understandably, deplore this width of doctrinal embrace, but in fact the very vagueness of so many in our church means that we are wide open in the

Church of England for the Spirit of God to move. The definiteness of Gospel doctrine comes as a breath of fresh air to renewed believers, and in many ways the hardest place for renewal to be experienced is in a legalistic, doctrinaire fellowship of traditional believers whose security is in their interpretation of truth rather than in the Spirit of God's revealing of all the open promises of Scripture.

However, it is also true to say that where well-taught Christians in a congregation do open up to a movement of the Spirit in renewal, the strongly scriptural setting of our Church of England worship means that there is a check on eccentricity and extreme expressions on spirituality, and there is a depth of mutual ministry that a relatively untaught congregation cannot know. When I was speaking to a gathering of priests at Westminster Cathedral many commented that in the Roman Catholic Church at that time a number of priests were renewed and individuals in their congregations shared the experience. They found it hard to lead the whole congregation into renewal, as has happened here and there in the Church of England. A godly Abbot, who was present, suggested that it was because for years their congregations had been familiar with sacramental worship but they had not had a tradition of Bible teaching. In this respect Anglicans value their heritage.

On the other hand, Tom Smail, former Director of the Fountain Trust and a respected leader in Renewal, shared recently that in the Church of England he so valued, the tradition of sacramental worship is expressed more frequently than in the church tradition to which he formerly belonged. In the Renewal movement many churches have found the fullness of a new tradition where both the preaching of the word verbally and the proclaiming of the word visually in the Sacraments are equally valued. No longer do we find scattered unprepared thoughts offered in the sermon slot in a renewal congregation. It is a time for feeding, teaching and meditating on God's word to us. No longer do we find a hastily, dutiful, tagged on celebration of the Holy Communion after the main event of Morning or Evening Prayer. If it still occurs at that point in worship it is now seen as a valued climax to worship, not just of the faithful few but for the majority of God's people who come to be gathered around the Lord's Table on the Lord's Day.

It is then that God moves—in the obedience of his people's prayerful togetherness. In Harborne we find that though we do not have 'servers' in the old sense, many people are used in the administration of the sacrament, and this pictures for the congregation the availability of our elders, staff and other leaders to serve the whole congregation in prayer, counselling and deliverance ministry. Often it is at such times that deep healing takes place, and though we have set up eldership and home group structures for ongoing ministry and counselling as a regular part of our life, it is often when the congregation is gathered for Sunday worship or at our midweek 'Open to God' meeting that God moves in power in people's lives. The emphasis on togetherness is important for us, as it was in the Acts of the Apostles for the early church (Acts 1:14; 2:1; 2:42, 44; 4:24 etc), and though one and another may exercise direct spiritual gifts of the Spirit, as the whole congregation gathers the renewal emphasis on every member ministry is perceived.

I have not dwelt on specific spiritual gifts, though these are thought by many to be a vital aspect of renewal. In fact in our congregation we do not talk about them very much because the Spirit directs us to centre on Jesus Christ and obedience to him. However, they are experienced and released among us in a multiplicity of situations by a large variety of people. The New Testament emphasizes the plurality of gifts (see the list in 1 Corinthians 12:4–11), 'varieties of gifts, service and working' (1 Cor 12:4–6), all being poured out in us and through us by the Spirit after God's heart of love was torn apart for us when Jesus his only Son died on the cross. Many people think that renewal brings division to the church. This word 'varieties' (which means to be 'torn assunder') is the only reference to division in relation to God's renewing work. This whole passage speaks rather of a new unity that the spirit brings to God's renewed people by 'the same Spirit, the same Lord, the same God' (1 Cor 12:4–6). This juxtaposition of unity and variety is highlighted in verse 11: 'all these [gifts] are inspired by one and the same Spirit, who apportions to each one individually as he wills.'

Renewal is not about sitting in church playing with gifts as children play with their birthday toys, however. In Ephesians 4:11 Paul speaks of men and women as God's gift to the church: 'some apostles, some prophets, some evangelists, some pastors and teachers, to equip the saints for the work of ministry.' Here again the Church of England with its parochial system is in a uniquely privileged position for reaching out in evangelism—a taught, Spirit-strengthened company of people reaching out 'to teach others also' (2 Tim 2:2). In the past, gospel preaching churches have been renowned for door-to-door visiting, open air preaching, parish missions, guest services and the use of evangelistic films. A renewed congregation has its own evangelistic impetus as people are drawn into church and are overwhelmed by the sense of the power and presence of God in the midst of his people. Furthermore, instead of a few individuals plodding wearily around the parish grieving that others do not join them, in a renewed fellowship a variety of people can take part as various tasks are allotted to them according to gifts and abilities. Some will emerge as front-line communicators manifesting a real gift of evangelism. Some will share in the work of administration, some will pray, others will open their homes for the witness team and yet others will offer to babysit. At times in our parish we have been able to establish a link between young mothers on the witness team who visit our afternoon home groups for the elderly with their babies or toddlers. A prayer partnership is thus formed between the oldest and the youngest in the congregation. Age barriers are broken and even the infirm can share in the evangelistic task. The joy of the parochial situation is that as the vicar has 'the cure of souls' there is in many parishes a sort of residual expectancy that someone from the parish church will visit one day, and in the power of the Spirit good things will happen.

God's sense of humour is also discovered. At one stage as we waited on God, we were despondent about the total disinterest and apathy in our patch of Birmingham. Someone gave a word urging us to pray that people walking along the streets and living in the homes of our parish should grow more and more miserable until they come to realize that they are indeed 'miserable sinners' and turn to God in repentance and faith. Late one evening, two of our burly men on the witness team made their last call on a person they knew from our records to be an elderly lady living on her own. She opened the door and having been warned by a previous letter put through her door, welcomed them warmly. That was amazing in itself at such a late hour in darkest Birmingham. She said: 'Do come in. I'm so glad to see you. I don't know why it is, but just recently I have been growing more and more miserable, and I believe you've got the answer for me.' With a wink and a nod our two men acknowledged God's answer to prayer and got on with the task of evangelism.

However, such work had not always been successful. Quite early on in our experience of renewal we had been led to ask why there was so much misunderstanding when God's word was preached and why so many people misinterpreted each other within the fellowship. After prayer and specific discernment we were shown elements of the spiritual battle raging behind the scenes as the 'god of this world blinded the minds of unbelievers' (2 Cor 4:4). Only Satan wants 'to keep them from seeing the light of the gospel of the glory of Christ' (v.5) and we found ourselves called to pray against a local spiritist group. Since that time hundreds of people have been converted at guest services and some through the witness team too. The total prayer life of the whole church has thus been fundamental to the task of evangelism and without the discernment through the release of spiritual gifts we might have toiled fruitlessly and preached with little effort for many years. If the long-standing parochial links that many have in the Church of England prove to be of tremendous evangelistic benefit to the church, the reality of long term spiritual opposition is also a factor in gospel warfare. When Christians are renewed in any church the spiritual conflict intensifies and the promise of Christ's victory must be claimed. He said to his disciples: 'Behold I have given you authority to tread upon serpents and scorpions, and over all the power of the enemy' (Lk 10:19). Mercifully he adds: 'and nothing shall hurt you'.

Looking at Renewal in the church, some perceive it as a superficial matter of tambourine bashing or swinging from the chandeliers within a high experience of charismatic praise. For us it's about God—his gracious Spirit's workings and gifts and love outpoured (Rom 5:5). It's about believing in his promises that we might know 'what are the riches of his glorious inheritance in the saints, and what is the immeasurable greatness of his power in us who believe' (Eph 1:18, 19). We want God's church to come out of the traction age, to cease being a lumbering giant, moving slowly and awkwardly, with great noise and much excess steam, and to move into an age of power and efficiency; to progress speedily in the task of worldwide evangelism in the power of the Spirit. For us in a parish church which has the words of the most primitive New Testament creed carved in beautifully huge letters above our Holy Table, it is supremely a matter of obedience. 'Jesus is Lord.'

Jesus is Lord! How can we refuse that call? How can we reject his gifts and power for service offered to us by his Spirit? How can we fail to have produced in our lives the qualities and characteristics of Jesus himself (Gal 5:22, 23) as the Holy Spirit produces ninefold fruit in our lives? Our prayer must be that of our *ASB* Rite A Thanksgiving—Lord, 'renew us by your Spirit'.

9

DEFENDING THE INSTITUTION

by

June Osborne[*]

I am a first-generation Anglican. I cannot remember meeting an Anglican (if you exclude the clergyman who baptized me at six weeks old) until I formed a firm friendship with the daughter of a vicar in my mid-teens. Not that I was unaware of the church. There was the Zion Congregationalist building which loomed over my junior school and smelt of dead mice. Several of my playfriends were used to going to church pretty regularly. But they were taught that it was a sin against the Virgin Mary to whistle or chew gum and, since I did both, it certainly prejudiced me in my judgement! At home my parents rarely spoke of 'the church', but when they did it was in an offhand, dismissive type of way—the way they might have referred to the House of Commons. It was a fact of life, but irrelevant to the world we inhabited. Like any institution it was part of the fabric of society, but it seemed to promote images and understandings of that society completely alien to our own.

Today I have pastoral charge of a parish where I sense that story repeated in the looks and words of my parishioners. I am once again living in an inner-city area where the church is

[*]June Osborne is a deaconess who served in the parishes of St Aldate's, Oxford and St Martin-in-the-Bullring, Birmingham before she was appointed Minister-in-Charge of St Mark's Old Ford in East London. She is a member of General Synod and serves on the Board for Social Responsibility. She is a Director of the annual Greenbelt Festival which draws up to 30,000 every August. She is married to a barrister and supports Manchester City!

fragile and trying hard not to be irrelevant to the life of the community. The twenty years in between have seen me become a Christian, encounter the church and its unwillingness to accept much of what is intrinsic to me, become an enthusiastic and committed Anglican, experience a call to both ministry and priesthood, and enjoy the rewards of living out that parish ministry alongside God's people. But the roots of that early story have never left me.

I said that the church felt like an 'institution' to my family. That means a large organization with strict hierarchies, rules of membership, loyalty to an established order and run by a centralized bureaucracy. Many young people are intensely critical of a church marked by such characteristics. Instead of nurturing personal relationships with Christ it seems rather to undermine growth and mission. This leads many to long for a different kind of church, one more 'responsive to the call of God's Spirit', one with greater immediacy and with the scope to become an 'alternative community'. There is sharp disapproval of the mainstream denominations. The argument is that they have conformed so much to the way of the world that they have lost their way. Doctrinal uncertainty is pointed to as only one symptom of such a state of affairs.

On the other hand the church, any part of the church, is not just an assembly of individuals all pursuing their own private faith. However painful it has been to work out commitment to the church, I have been kept by a sense that in the corporate Christian experience there is a treasure store unavailable to the solitary Christian. Indeed, it is a vital route out of the infernal aspects of the individualism of our age. The Bible has new things to show us if we read it remembering the way God worked, not just with individuals, but also through communities. But just like those biblical communities, the church today fights between life and death. Life is the vision of a world in God's image, pledged to his priorities and reflecting his nature. Death is the way of self-interest, holding on to fears and prejudices, putting your own survival before the aims which ought to motivate you. It is a struggle which every institution faces. How often does one come across an organization or club which started off with great ambitions, but now seems to exist only for the sake of keeping going? Unless we are going to opt out and live our faith in the narrowness of private life, we are all going to face the same demand. We are partners of the Spirit in redeeming the groups we belong to just as much as we long for the personal transformation of individuals. The two are often linked. A church owning an attractive faith is surely going to have to ensure the integrity of its own inner life. And that church which puts its vision for God's kingdom before all else will be able to show individuals the way to life.

I do not believe that the church needs to be rescued from being an 'institution'. The task is not to dismantle an institution, for church history tells us that like the man who swept his life clean of one spirit, we may well find seven others appearing! Instead we have to ask ourselves: 'How does the church commit itself to a transforming vision rather than merely pursuing its own survival? How do we ensure that our vision and energy is building a church of mission and not sacrificing all to maintenance?' With such commitments the church does not cease to be an institution, but it ceases to serve its own needs and knows itself as an organ which serves the people who gather for worship and witness and those who live within its influence.

I wouldn't be an Anglican if I did not believe the Church of England capable of such a vision. But it has to be won and protected. We need to go on shaping our lives as instruments of that vision. It means practical change and personal cost. To put flesh on the bones of that sentence let me share some of the places I believe the Church of England needs to be willing to either strengthen good practice, or change to a better way.

Structures

An important starter question for any group of people—a family, a Bible-study group, a community centre or tennis club, a multinational corporation, is: 'Where does the power lie?' The church has to accept that it will be known and judged for what it has to say about power.

It is the image of the Church of England as a vastly power-ful body which lingers around too many people's minds. The Church Commissioners are equated with the Gnomes of Zurich and the bishops with crown princes. It feels like the church of the rich and the educated. Yet we pay homage to a gospel which challenges power for its own sake and trades in a different currency of worth. It is a gospel of love, and love has to include just distribution of power. How can our structure be true to that? What limits do we need to set on our behav-iour and attitudes which will redistribute our power in the way we would like? How can we direct our resources so that they are neither squandered nor left to collect dust, but rather mobilized and shared?

What kind of church do we want to be?

We were on holiday with a baptist minister and her husband. In our conversations she frequently referred to her life in 'the parish', and there was much teasing about her use of such an Anglican phrase. The concept of the parish is often laughed about, and frequently resented, but it is where we begin and end. What kind of church do we want to be? The answer is always the same—a local church. A church built on the day-to-day lives of ordinary Christians. A church accessible and available to anyone and everyone. A church which is bound up with the experience of a community, the stories of unex-ceptional people. All the structures of Anglicanism in the end focus on that unit of worship; they should all be accountable to the mission of daily life. For God asks structures and organizations to serve the human story, and 'church' does not exist except where God is at work in that story.

That is not to say that other denominations don't have the same relationship to a local community, but there is a unique commitment embodied in the parish structure. In part it helps each individual Christian live a more integrated life and build an empathy between their place of residence and their spiritual goals. When I moved into this parish the congrega-tion of the church was tiny, if determined. Before long I had met nearly two dozen Christians who live within a mile of our home but who worship at large, eclectic churches in the centre of London. What was worse, most of them seemed to be musicians yet we are still without a pianist! That contrast is not about people rejecting a dead local church, but rather about the way people in our society live disintegrated lives with their home, work, church and citizenship all inhabiting different areas. A church which worships where it lives can at least begin realistic bridge-building. Maybe even more important, the parish says something vital about the relationship of local people to the Christian faith.

Who belongs?

To whom does the local church belong? The Anglican answer includes not only the regular worshippers at a church building, but everyone who lives within the parish boundaries. That boundary is, of course, artificial but it may alert us to other more invisible boundaries which are far more deadly. One of the most entrenched beliefs about the church is that there are insiders—those acceptable because of their dress, or lifestyle, or status; and outsiders—which is everyone else. Outsiders feel that they have not made the grade and are therefore excluded. However much we voice regret about such feelings they will only be reinforced if our structures give the impression that we exist for the benefit of the club members. I grew up hearing persistent criticism of the 'woolly edges' of Anglicanism, the lack of commitment of 'nominal Christianity'. But I have to confess that I have gained more insights from the people who inhabit those 'woolly edges', who are either on their way into, or out of, the church and from people of entirely different spiritualities than from all the voices that seem at first glance to be more 'sound'.

Some will think that Anglican structures lack any discrimination, for instance in the baptism policy, but I know how easy it is to want to become protectionist. I begin to want to set entrance exams for the church which speak not of the hospitality of a generous God but of the meanness of judgemental people. The church is certainly not the church of the rich and the educated but neither is it the church of a Christian sub-culture or the place where only Christians, as we define them, can enter. It is the place where power of all kinds is questioned in order to be genuinely shared, and where everyone ought to know they belong.

Spirituality

Most of the teaching and training of my early Christian years led me to believe that spirituality, the knowing of God, is an intensely private affair—done in a closet away from the strivings of the world. It has the quality expressed in the popular hymn:

Take from our souls the strain and stress
And let our ordered lives confess
The beauty of Thy peace.

In a sense that is true. Our spirituality is there to give us perspective so that we may see the world through God's eyes. It was not the personal aspect I started to question, but there was a steadily growing unease with pietism—spirituality in a vacuum—away from the influence and injuries of the world. It felt as if I'd been asked to pray with my back to the world, something Jesus never did. Just as he carried with him his family, his nation's history, his class, occupations, sex, personality and calling so I began to accept that those aspects of my 'story' were going to interact with how I saw God, how he spoke to me and how I saw myself in relation to him. It was that which first attracted me so strongly to Anglicanism. I felt that it gave me permission to express my personal and cultural experience as it was, and to work out how it related to traditional beliefs about God and the world, rather than asking it to instantly conform to pre-moulded images.

The three strong foundations of Anglican doctrine and living—the bedrock biblical authority, traditions of the living church and the conscience of the individual Christian—give all that is needed to stay on the right track. With them we can journey into new experiences and ideas, interact with any class or culture, establish fresh patterns and know all is held in Christ's lordship.

That freedom to know Christ speaking differently into our experience brings hope and confidence. Let me give just two examples from my own past and present.

I was chaplain of a children's hospital for four years during which time I saw hundreds of children fight for health, and parents struggle with anxiety or even bereavement. My spirituality did not equip me for the task because I had been taught to 'trust and obey'. I'd been given a sense of guilt about failure, negative emotions and inadequacy; and here I was surrounded by all of them! I had to learn how to be angry with God, how to pray when you have no words and how to rest content with just being there, unable to do anything. I was grateful for the spiritual resources that came from parts of the church better at such skills than evangelicalism. In time I had to change how I thought about God, what I thought prayer was about and what I was doing in the world. It felt so very threatening at the beginning, but now I see how God was ahead of me, sufficient for everything I felt and encountered.

Our spirituality not only meets our moments of crisis or change, it also interacts with who we are. That includes our sexuality and a central issue for the church of our time is to hear what women have to say about their sense of self, their spirituality. We are asked to respond to their request that our shared life should not make masculine spirituality the starting point. It has not been easy to live with the knowledge that it has too often been the church which is reluctant to hear what women want and instead has retreated into unreal convictions and outmoded clichés. This is especially sad since so many Christian women are motivated by a real desire to carry the gospel faith into all areas of their life. That can only be done by they themselves—no one discovers how God is real for someone else. And we will have new riches, new insights, new mistakes to offer out of our experience of liberation, out of the spirituality we own.

Perhaps the debate about women's ordination has decoyed us from seeing the whole landscape of women's spirituality yet to be won. Perhaps the climate of the women's movements has made us feel uncomfortable or threatened. But what women are doing is no different from what Paul did when he carried the gospel to the Gentiles. It is carrying the reality of Christ into another realm of human experience and asking what Christian loyalty means. If it is in the nature of the gospel to declare fit what the world calls unfit, surely it is appropriate for women to at least question a limited or ill-fitting spirituality?

It would hardly seem that the Anglican Church is happy to encourage such questioning. The synodical agenda of the 1980s is streaked through with slow-moving legislation about the role of women, all of it controversial and accompanied by much pain. It is with awareness of all that, and the crucial impact on my own future ministry, that I can still say that the Church of England is a good place for a woman to be! In the search for a spirituality which fits, be it struggling with suffering or sexuality, there are pieces of Anglican scaffolding which are not only supportive but also help in the design.

I have mentioned the rich traditions which are available to us, providing a sense of spiritual history, a source of nourishment, a stimulus to pray as you can and not as you can't. My love-hate relationship with liturgy has always left me grateful that it isn't all down to my inadequate imagination or just one generation's perspective. The same mixture is there in the relationship between doctrine and worship. Belonging to a credal church, where belief is staunchly biblical but always tied and applied to the worshipping life of today's Christians is another piece of the scaffolding. What I believe has been fought out and called orthodox by past saints, but it is lived in today's culture. Maybe it is the indigenous, wide-ranging presence of the Church of England, maybe it is the diversity within a firm structure, maybe it is the openness of entry. Whatever the reason, there is an understanding at the heart of Anglicanism that the gospel is separate from the culture and a determination not to confuse the two. We are part of a communion which spans the world and what is faithfulness for a Maori bishop will not be the same as for a New Jersey lay-woman. What is common is that they journey knowing that what is unchanging is God's character, presence, effect and assurance.

Service

A contradiction I encountered early in my discovery of Anglicanism was that of leadership and service. I had been told that Anglicans believed in 'one-man ministry', whereas the churches I had thus far attended were invested in 'every-member ministry'. The question of robes was usually cited as an example of this exaltation of the priest as all-powerful. The reality has been different in every Anglican church known to me. I don't doubt that some people leave theological college believing in their own self-importance, but real leadership blossoms in service. Real service is not so much about church committees as interdependence. Interdependence is ministry *between* people not just servicing the 'vicar's needs'.

It's a false contrast to set 'every-member ministry' over and against strong, identifiable leadership. When I take the lead I do so on behalf of the people around me. We complement each other's skills. We know each other's blind spots. We expect each other to contribute according to our needs. It is every bit a team operation and there are all the frustrations and weaknesses you would expect. Far from setting me apart from people my robes remind me and them that the leadership I exercise is not a 'one-woman authority' but is given me in their name.

Seeing interdependence at work has also enriched my models of authority. Too often the church associates authority with hierarchy, discipline and status. Too often ignored is the authority of ministries which arise out of God's gifts given in unassuming corners. We have a woman in our congregation who has a gift of evangelism so natural she hardly knows she's doing it! She would be embarrassed if I put so grand a name to what is second nature to her. Now I would be very foolish to ignore the authority she has as her instincts and leadership in that area far outstrip mine.

Likewise there is the authority of confessors in the church. Listening to those people and parts of the church in situations where they must bear witness, often at great cost. It might be a young teenager in a hostile family, it might be a bishop in South Africa. Theirs is the authority of living close to hard questions, and teaching us when the gospel is in jeopardy.

There is also the authority of our corporate life—we are 'members one of another'. This is the authority the Archbishop's Commission on Urban Priority Areas calls us back to. The hold which different parts of the church have on each other because we are one in Christ—in this case the hold the urban has on the suburban.

There are many more sources of authority in our life together. Far from being an outdated institution the Church of England literally hums with inter-relationships which tell us loud and clear that God is at work. Being a national church in a multi-cultural society such as this has ultimately to speak of relationship—if we reflect and represent all sections of our community we mirror the service of Christ which was able to cross all boundaries. If we are bound by allegiance stronger than likemindedness we mirror the strength of the gospel. If we catch hold of the coat tails of the Spirit and keep clear the vision, ancient institutions will be transformed in the name of the kingdom and continue to be agents of hope.

10

YOUNG PEOPLE AND THE CHURCH

by

Julia Wills*

The past

As you begin to read this chapter, memories of teenage and young adult years happily dominated by involvement with the church may be flooding your mind. The middle years of the twentieth century were years when the church was often the centre of social activity in the local community. It was the natural gathering place for large groups of young people. Many Christian marriages first blossomed at the church Youth Club.

This attractiveness of the church to young people was probably even more notable in evangelical churches. Here, far from being put off by the firm discipline of regular quiet times and the authoritarian denial of many of the pleasures of life such as dancing and the cinema, young people were apparently challenged and drawn by this strict rule of life.

The pillars of today's church are more often than not people who shared in those happy days of the church Youth Club. And it is clear that those years were important, formative years in their Christian growth.

---

*Julia Wills is Diocesan Youth Officer for the Diocese of Leicester and Religious Programmes Producer for BBC Radio Leicester. Before that, for six years, she was Diocesan Youth Officer in the Birmingham Diocese. She has worked with various groups of people producing Bible study material for young people and is at present writing a booklet of creative Bible study based on John's Gospel for the Bible Society. In the distant past she was a member of the Youth Fellowship run by the editor of this book!

The present

So what went wrong? What has happened in the last twenty to twenty-five years to cause the demise of that apparently indestructible social force? There is no denying it, *the church Youth Club is not what it used to be.*

Certainly there *are* pockets of strength, but it is often difficult to discern whether they are signs of hope or remnants of a past which has not yet realized that its time is gone.

Again, the strength of Christian youth work is more apparent in the evangelical wing of the church. It is still there that greater numbers of committed and growing young Christians are evident; and that *must* be a sign of hope.

But there is another side of the coin. On the whole it cannot be denied that the majority of those young people belong to a single type. Generally 'successful' youth groups are formed by middle class, articulate young people.

A few years ago I held a consultation with young people. Clergy from the thirteen deaneries were asked to send representatives. It was a very diverse diocese, a large inner city area with satellite council housing estates and a lower number of salubrious suburban areas. Most of the deaneries sent three or four representatives, which encouraged me. 'Aha,' I thought, 'this time we'll get real young people; true Brummies.'

As they arrived I was slightly disconcerted by the number of times I heard such comments as 'Sue! What are *you* doing here?' or 'Paul! I didn't know you were coming!'. When we sat down for our first session we discovered that out of the forty participants a good 50% came from two of the independent grammar schools.

'Why,' I asked them in despair, 'do all the Christians in this place come from the grammar schools?'

They considered this for a while and eventually agreed that it was only articulate young people who bothered to ask questions about 'life, the universe and everything'.

Certainly we need to acknowledge and appreciate the strength and value of our work with those articulate, middle-class young people. It is good that, faced with a challenge they take it up and seek to make it their own. Young people are not trammelled by thoughts of churchmanship, the right approach, the correct words. They are excited by the offer of new life, and enthused by the desire to change the world! Just as perhaps their parents did before them, these young people are challenged by the discipline and direction of the church. Together they find strength to face the world and to confront the animosity and perhaps apathy of their peers.

But there is a danger in that solidarity. In standing together and standing apart, it is easy to stand aloof, unaware of the reality of what life is like at the cutting edge. Often, when teaching these young people what the Bible says, we omit to equip them for how it really applies to the 'world out there'.

However, I don't want to knock good, strong Christian youth work. At worst it at least gives young people a code by which to live and at best it throws up many thousands of leaders, counsellors, pastors and evangelists in a world which needs them. It certainly attempts to direct young people into the way of following Jesus Christ.

But what else of the present youth scene in the church? In my seven years as a youth officer in the Midlands I have seen much to depress, but also lights in the darkness.

The cry which comes from many churches is: 'We can't keep them, confirmation is like a passing out parade—they get "done" and then they go, never to darken the door again'.

It has to be admitted that the majority of young people in our churches are children of church-going parents. It often seems as if confirmation is the last ditch stand of parents who have wielded the Sunday attendance stick for years. 'When you've been confirmed, you can decide for yourself'—and they do; a lie-in, the school football/hockey team or homework usually wins.

One group of parents I met recently blamed it all on the school system. 'They don't teach religion any more, so the kids grow up not knowing what it's all about.' My view is that often Sunday-by-Sunday exposure to the sort of joyless 'worship' which I have sometimes been obliged to attend has taken its toll. If that is Christianity, they want nothing more to do with it.

What sort of message are young people hearing from the church? And how are they hearing that message?

I was invited recently to meet with a group of young people involved in a local church to find out from them what, if anything, they would like in terms of 'extra worship' activities from the church. By involved, I mean that some sang in the choir, others were bell-ringers and others were just leaving Sunday School.

We played some games and did some exercises, to encourage discussion about what made life enjoyable and what they thought about the church. There was quite a bit of laughter and chat until I said 'And would you like to learn about Jesus?' It was as if someone had turned the power off! Suddenly the shutters went up over their faces and there was deadly silence. I tried putting the words in a different order and used different sentences until, out of pity, one of them said 'That's so *boring*'. The cry of youth! But until the mention of the One who said he came to bring life in all its fullness, that word had not been heard.

If they were not being taught about Christianity in school, there would seem to be only one other place where they might have picked up that message—church.

'It's all very well,' you may be saying, 'but it was pretty boring in my day as well, but *I* stuck it out.' So you did. And all power to you. But the world and the educational system in which today's young people are growing up is different.

Television has radically altered the attention span and interest level of young people. It isn't even possible to listen to a piece of music these days without the ubiquitous music video to accompany it. We are living in an instant and visual age. It's not the fault of our younger generation that they need constant stimulation and ever more sophisticated 'entertainment' to enable learning. If blame is to be meted out, then it must be laid fairly and squarely on the shoulders of the adult society who are the ones who have instilled the message into our young people.

Even then it is not just teachers or advertisers who are to blame. Another group of parents were discussing young people's values and the fact that their children took so many good things in life for granted. Slowly the truth began to dawn; if their children had received from birth all the advantages that they themselves had been denied, then *why should* the young people see those advantages as privileges to be valued? They were more to be regarded as rights. So why were they as parents surprised, when their children demanded more or held what they had in low esteem?

It is clear that our style of sharing the message must be reconsidered. Not, I hasten to add, watered down; more pointed up, illustrated, shown to be relevant to real lives and present day concerns. We must find attractive ways of presenting the gospel and we must allow young people the space to ask questions.

Even if we have managed to share a gospel which speaks to young people and holds them, we often still fail to incorporate them fully into the family of the church.

How often I remember as a teenager being told by well-meaning adult members of the congregation, 'You'll understand when you grow up.'

I confess I still gloat a little over one particular incident when at the age of seventeen I was a PCC member. During a discussion about a proposed church extension building scheme I had the timerity to suggest that we went ahead in faith and trusted God to help us raise the finance! I was quickly put in my place by the local millionaire who told me, kindly, that I was a little too young to understand such financial matters. I gave him the benefit of the doubt since by then I hadn't reached my first £100, let alone a million! However, *seven years later* they did indeed decide to go ahead in faith. By then, through inflation, an extra £50,000 had been added to the bill!

There were probably very good reasons for the hesitation. The point I wish to make is that, by keeping young people quiet until they think like we do, we ensure a church which will always run the risk of being bogged down in the status quo. We are afraid to take risks or to try again when something fails. How often have you heard the phrase 'We tried that once but it didn't work'? I have observed that often, when young people really have been fired with enthusiasm and have accepted Jesus into their lives, they in their naivety actually *believe* what they have been taught about faith and prayer. The challenge they pose to the adults or more 'mature' members of the church is more than we can cope with. Perhaps that is what Jesus meant, when he said 'Unless you become like little children, you shall not enter the kingdom of God'.

Not, of course, that I would want to preclude the possibility of the movement of the Holy Spirit. But then, in some of the churches I have visited, members are so busy maintaining tradition that the Holy Spirit, like young people, is more likely to be told to 'wait until you've grown up' as well!

What can we do?

So where *is* the hope for the Church of England in our work with young people? Where do we need to be directing our attention?

Security The characteristic of adolescence is the desire to break away from the home, to establish an independent identity and to become an adult. But the process of breaking away is in itself frightening and disconcerting. Young people need someone, something, to kick against *'safely'*. Probably, deep down, the most important thing about breaking away is having somewhere to come back to.

The Family has in the past been seen as the bastion of security, the one place where you don't need to pretend, where mum and dad are there to support and protect.

The latest statistics on marriage breakdown suggest that almost one in three marriages end in divorce. A happy and secure marriage is almost more of the exception than the rule. Children are often the unhappy pawns in the 'tug of love' between parents, caught in a crisis of loyalty and consequently feeling that they belong nowhere, to no one.

What can the church say or do in that situation? Of course, our teaching on marriage and support of couples in trouble is invaluable. But what of the children caught in the middle?

I run many training courses for youth leaders and 'those who are interested'. Often on those courses I meet women in their mid-40s who say 'I'm not really a youth leader, I just love the kids and make the coffee'. It often becomes clear that those ladies are the ones who hear all the joys and sorrows of the young people, poured out over a cup of coffee. There are others, almost surrogate parents, in the church who open their homes and hearts to young people. We need to seek out those people and encourage their very real and important ministry.

Unemployment is the 'bogey man' of our present age. I have heard of at least one third year class of young people being told by the teacher 'It doesn't really matter what "O" levels you do because only about two out of the thirty of you will get a job.' What hope is there for a 14-year-old hearing that? Where is the motivation even to try?

Ours is truly a divided society—there are those young people who don't care at all about school, work or the future, and have given up completely. And there are those on the verge of breakdowns, suffering from the torment of parental pressure to pass exams and succeed. Even if they do get through the exams and go to university, there is no guarantee of a job at the end.

So we are faced with two dilemmas, one practical and the other philosophical.

First things first; if young people are unemployed what do they *do* with themselves? Those of us fortunate enough to have moved from education into employment will know the value and formative nature of that first job. It was there that the bumptiousness of youth was rubbed off; there we learnt discipline, learnt the real independence and self-respect of having our *own* money, began to interact with members of another generation. All those advantages of employment are being denied young people—*they are being thrown into extended adolescence with no way out.* The church is one place where, in theory, members of all generations meet together. Here surely we can offer some positive experience of 'belonging', to young people who feel restless and alone.

Secondly, the question of philosophy. What values are we teaching our young people? Jesus told his disciples to give away everything, leave their jobs and follow him. Yet, how often in conversation with a stranger is our first question 'What do you do for a living?'—as if a job makes a person. How can we learn to value one another for *who* we are, and not for *what* we are?

The Iona Community in Glasgow is struggling with this issue in the poorest parts of Glasgow and Edinburgh. Young volunteers live together in small communities of three or four people in tenement flats. Most of them are on the dole, as are their neighbours. They are there seeking to identify with Christ in the community among the powerless and the poor. In their words they are seeking how to 'learn from the bottom, just as Christ himself did'.

In this way, the young people involved in the scheme not only learn about life which is far removed from their own background. They also learn about a new life-style which breaks the acquisitive materialistic mode on which so many young people have been encouraged to base their lives.

Their lives together are strengthened by weekly meetings for sharing and worship and a monthly celebration attended by many hundreds of young people with whom they have contact in the course of their 'witness' in the community.

But these young people still face misunderstanding from older people and the church. Why, when they are intelligent and capable, don't they get proper jobs and 'get on in life' like everyone else?

What are we doing in the church to change our attitudes, to break the line which says we must keep up with the Joneses; that says only work which brings in a good wage can also bring dignity?

The Future, for many young people, poses one of the greatest threats—not really because they are afraid of it but because they wonder if there will actually be one. Not all young people are active members of CND or its opposition, but most have an awareness of the threat of nuclear destruction.

One youth leader asked all the members of her club to bring to the next meeting a record which said something important to them. She was amazed to discover that every one of the records was about war or the end of the world.

Many of the adults in our churches have been through at least one, if not two, world wars. When young people express this fear, they often think them cowardly and lily-livered. But never before have we been faced with the possibility of total destruction.

If this is the sort of world in which young people are growing up, it's no wonder that many have almost given up hope. What is the church *being heard to say* about hope in our world?

How is the church reaching young people?

It is only too easy when thinking about outreach to give glib and easy answers. I know too many ministers who have been weighed down by the guilt of apparent failure to offer such answers. Each place is different, every person is different.

When all's said and done, missions are more easily conducted in middle-class areas. Supper parties, talks and Christian concerts are easier to stage in larger homes, with more articulate and more wealthy people.

It is more often the church in the inner city or on the satellite housing estate which struggles. For a start, there are usually far fewer people willing to take on a leadership role in any area of the life of the church even less so in organizing a mission.

Outreach among young people in these areas is often through the open youth club, where young people from the surrounding area gather to play snooker, table tennis, darts and other indoor games. Some of these clubs may have an 'epilogue' or something similar where the vicar or curate is often wheeled in to do his 'holy bit' while the young people stand around, shuffling and muttering and waiting to get back to their games. Or it may be that the leaders see the club itself and the fact that they are Christians as sufficient witness.

There are many very good clubs of this sort, where the leaders struggle against enormous odds in order to share something of the love of Jesus with the young people whom they serve. The trouble is that often the difficulties they face are increased by the conflict they often meet from the church itself.

I know of one club run by Christian youth leaders who shared their faith openly and often with their members. The club was regarded as one of the best in the city, and visitors from around the world were taken by the LEA to visit this impressive piece of church youth work. Young people were helped to leave a road to crime, many felt the club was more of a home to them than anywhere else and the leaders were much loved.

The church, on the other hand, did all they could to get rid of the club from their premises. Their church hall was getting bumped around and the kids didn't come to church.

There were faults on both sides; but I was still left wondering what Jesus would have said in that situation.

Youth work among non-church young people is long and hard. It is no longer possible to assume *any* biblical knowledge or church background. Parents no longer send their children to Sunday School for a bit of peace and quiet on a Sunday morning. There are plenty of other places for them to go. And as I've mentioned before, children are very rarely taught biblical studies at school.

We are, therefore, starting from scratch when we try to reach non-church young people. We *must* speak to them, in a language which they understand, about subjects which concern them.

What is more, the whole church community needs to be involved in that sharing of the gospel. We may not all be potential youth leaders. But we are all able to pray. If we believe in the power of prayer, what might happen in our open youth clubs if each member of the church became a 'prayer parent' of one or two members of the club? It would, of course, mean finding out about members of the club, talking with the youth leader, possibly (oh fear and dread!) even talking to the young person her- (or him-) self. If we are to reach young people in our community it must be in partnership.

We in the church are also very poor at enabling Christians really to *share* their faith or even to learn very much about it. In many churches, confirmation classes are the only formal training we have. The evangelical tradition of teaching sermons is invaluable but how do we actually equip and fire people to go out and share what they have learnt? If we are talking about reaching young people, then *the obvious evangelists for that task are young people themselves*. We need to find ways of helping them to have confidence in a dynamic faith and to challenge them with the command of Christ to 'go and make disciples of all people'. There are some good resources on the market these days which make Bible study much more fun, creative and, above all, challenging to young people. There are also agencies available to train leaders in the use of these materials. Diocesan Youth Officer, CYFA and Frontier Youth Trust are just three of the agencies available to assist and support youth leaders in their work.

How is the church welcoming young people?

It's all very well to talk about reaching young people but what happens when they actually respond and come into church? How are they welcomed? How are they integrated?

The worship in our churches is often the thorny issue. There are, thank goodness, some churches which seem to have got it right for the adults and young people who make up the congregations. Old and new mingle both reverently and joyfully and everyone goes away feeling that they have, in some way, offered their worship to God.

But there are many places where this is not the case, where battles are fought long and hard to keep the *Book of Common Prayer*. Young people and newcomers are expected to do a mental leap back 300 years to a language and form of activity totally alien to them. The problem is, of course, intensified in many places where large numbers of the population cannot read. How then can they be expected to follow an order of service?

Worship—important as it is—is not, however, the key to incorporating young people into the church. As in any organization it is much more to do with personal contact, the word of welcome, the smile of recognition and taking time to ensure that newcomers know their way around the order of service. I can hardly believe the number of times I have heard that the only words young people have had spoken to them on entering a church for the first time are 'Would you mind moving, please, you're sitting in my pew'!

Within two months of moving into a group of parishes one clergyman knew all the young people under his care and had opened his home to them. He takes them out on trips and for meals and is always available to them. Basically he is loving those young people into the kingdom. Of course we cannot all be like that, but we can all do our own small bit to open ourselves to love young people more. That may be by being a little more flexible in our approach to worship. It may be by digging more willingly into our pockets for repairs on the church hall. It may be by opening up our homes to young people.

After all we are called to be the family of God. Any parent knows just how much they are called to sacrifice for their children. If we truly want the best for the children of our world, we must be prepared to go that extra mile.

Work with young people in the church is very rarely easy. It is often frustrating, annoying and depressing. But it can also be great fun, very rewarding and exciting.

If there is to be hope for the Church of England it obviously doesn't lie solely in our work with young people. But if we don't take seriously the challenge posed to us by the younger generation in our world there is certainly a danger that the church will move further and further away from the possibility of touching their lives at any stage in the future.

This poem, written by a girl of 16, poses the challenge and the plea which we in the church would be foolish to ignore.

World, I am youth
Unsettled and searching,
Exploring the heights and the plain.
I wander your deserts, thirsty and pale,
I weep in the beating rain.
Ascend I the mountains with eagerness,
Hungry and seeking my goal.
Then into barbs of stinging thorns
I fall with deluded soul.
In your shadow of dust I tremble,
I fear death and even life.
Tomorrow I laugh and confidence
Pervades my daily strife.
World, I am youth
The hope of your day.
I am bewildered and young in this land.
I am searching your paths
For a vision called truth—
Give me your hand.

THE POLITICAL IMPERATIVE

by

Pete Broadbent[*]

Much has been written about the change in Church of England evangelicalism from a world-denying pietistic sect to a world-affirming diverse grouping concerned to play its full part in the church of the nation.[6] One specific spin-off from this change is the involvement of a large number of Anglican evangelicals in the world of politics and social action. What I want to do in this chapter is to map a fairly personal account of the experience of being a Christian in politics, to address the issues of theology and the practical problems that social involvement raises, and to plead that involvement in politics and social action really is an imperative for evangelicals in the Church of England.

Why did evangelicals suddenly begin, in the 1970s, to get politically involved? (Of course, political activity was nothing strange to nineteenth-century evangelicals such as Wilberforce or Shaftesbury.) First, the Reformed theology which proclaimed Christ as Lord of every aspect of human existence began to be taken seriously. Anglican evangelicals at Keele in 1967 had pronounced on the need to be involved in church

---

[*]Pete Broadbent is Anglican Chaplain to the Polytechnic of North London. He is a member of General Synod. Since 1982, he has been a Labour Councillor in the London Borough of Islington, and Chair of the Development and Planning Committee. Married to Sarah, with a seven-year-old son called Simon, he lives in Highbury and relaxes by listening to contemporary music and watching films. He admits to an irrational attachment to Tottenham Hotspur F.C.

and society, and it was Reformed theology which provided the tools for the task. The writings of Francis Schaeffer and the Dutch school of philosophy associated with Abraham Kuyper and Herman Dooyeweerd were particularly influential in helping Christians to see that no part of God's universe was outside his sovereignty and no human institution value-free in its presuppositions. It was up to Christians to emerge from their cultural ghetto and to reclaim human institutions as God's domain.

Secondly, I think that the generation of people who had grown up in the sixties saw politics and participation as a natural expression of their faith, because it was an important aspect of their lives anyway. Experiments with schools councils led into student union politics, which in turn led into community involvement. We were involved because we were children of a particular generation. My own personal pilgrimage, which is by no means unique, followed that pattern. It was natural to wrestle with the application of Christian faith to that aspect of life because it was such a major feature of life. So, for example, one might begin with the belief that students, as part of an educational institution, ought to be involved in shaping its decision-making.

Two major issues—the college's role as landowner of an area of the city which it wanted to redevelop as a shopping centre (which would require the destruction of a large area of housing), and the question of whether the institution should admit women—were on the agenda. At a naive level, it seemed appropriate to question the morality of the shopping scheme, and to argue for the justice of equality of educational opportunity. But how could such opinions be expressed and aired? What role might Christians in the college have? Should they act corporately? Was there a need to find someone to act as a representative of their views? Christians in the college were politicized by the experience, got involved in the student union, elected a Christian as student union president, and grappled with the fact that they were no longer just a group of people committed to a particular style of personal evangelism (though they *were* still committed to evangelism!), but had become Christian social activists.

A third factor to set alongside the theological motivation and instinctive involvement is the fact that 'single issue' politics came very much to the fore in that period. Feminism, apartheid, racism, and nuclear weapons and their implications for the totality of society and the church could not be ignored. The pressing urgency for those who called themselves disciples of Jesus Christ to deal with these issues pushed many who might not be 'political' in the 'party' sense of that word into the arena of social action.

So much for history. Evangelicals, perhaps belatedly, got involved in politics. (By politics I mean any form of collective action by which people organize themselves to achieve a common end, whether school parents' association, community group, or political party). They found they needed two things: a theological framework within which to operate, and an understanding of the way in which personal political involvement related to the structures and life of the church. Other spiritual traditions, such as the Catholic wing of the Church of England, had a much longer, noble history of social involvement, and a theological framework to offer, but it seemed important to work up a distinctively evangelical theology. It also became clear that there was a need to link the theology with the church—specifically the Church of England, within which many, though not all, found themselves operating. That brought particular questions, such as the role of the parish church in social affairs, and the function of being the Established Church in relation to having a political role—questions which have been sharpened up considerably by the debate of the last five years between Church and Government.

It is important too to avoid merely baptizing one party political viewpoint with a highly selective series of texts and calling that a theological framework. The Bible needs to be interpreted more carefully than that. What theological framework can appropriately inform the Christian who is involved in social action?

Our mandate for social involvement starts with our concept

of mission. The words of the risen Jesus to his disciples—
'Peace be with you. As the Father sent me, so I send you' (Jn
20:21)—provide the basis for mission. We, as disciples of the
Jesus who was sent with good news in word and deed, walk in
the shoes of our master (for that is what discipleship means).
We are sent to the world as he was. Evangelism and social
action, the twin prongs of mission, are our calling. But we
need to expand on this, and evolve a whole Bible perspective.

The *createdness* of humanity in God's image (Gen 1:27–28)
will provide a starting-point. Human beings, made to reflect
God's character, with a mandate for the stewardship of the
created order, are also human beings who are fallen (Gen
3:1–21). They experience radical alienation from their creator,
and participate in the radical alienation of the entire universe,
which groans as it waits for its liberation (Rom 8:20–22).

The *incarnation* will inform our thinking, as we realize that
the Jesus whom we follow is God incarnate—God took flesh,
and in doing so affirmed the value of humankind in a way that
points to the ultimate transfiguration of humanity to perfection which will occur at the end of time. Most pertinently,
God incarnate points us away from the unhappy dualism of
body and spirit that has perverted Christian theology for too
long, and reminds us that the Hebrew concept of the person as
unity is the biblical idea upon which Christian theology is
based. So, *a Christian taking the incarnation seriously will take
the life of this world seriously, for it was on this stage that the
Word became flesh.*

The *kingdom of God* plays an ever-increasing role in
political theology, as the radical kingdom, which has invaded
this world in the person of Jesus Christ, takes root among us
and points to the future perfect kingdom through signs of
the justice and peace which will one day characterize the
redeemed creation of the new heavens and the new earth. The
kingdom is neither a place nor an institution, but is simply
where the rule of God is seen in the lives of individuals and
society.

An understanding of the Old Testament ideas of justice and
peace will also have an important part to play.[7] The character

of God demands justice in his world. The ordering of society and the laws of God expressed in (for example) the Ten Commandments can only be seen in the overall context of a God who demands justice from all people, and not merely from those in covenant relationship with him. Once this is recognized, political relationships become a crucial aspect of our response to God's demands. To speak of a bias to the materially poor, or to argue that the kingdom of God is of necessity concerned with justice in economic relationships is only a logical extension of this Old Testament insight.

A wide theology of *redemption* will also give us cause for hope in the future of creation. Paul writes in Colossians 1:20 that 'God made peace through his sacrificial death on the cross and so brought back to himself all things, both on earth and in heaven.' That statement, that in the cross there is redemption for the created order as well as for individual human beings, is one which points to a future hope for the universe. It gives us cause to believe that the cataclysmic alienation of the fall is to be reversed. The cross also points to the element of *suffering* which is inherent in Christian social action. No Christian theology which does not take seriously the fact that we as followers of Christ are called to a life which is marked by suffering and the cross (1 Pet 2:21) can claim to be authentic.

Resurrection will similarly inform our politics as we recognize that the new hope to which Christians are called transcends the distinction of the this-worldly/other-worldly—and that the eternal life of Christ is one which straddles the grave. We live the life of the resurrection now 'in sure and certain hope of the resurrection to eternal life'—and that means we can neither ignore the circumstances of the physical world in which we live this earthly life, nor forget that our calling is to a life beyond, in the consummated kingdom of God.

It is important to note that this biblical framework does not constitute a political manifesto or an ideology. What it does is to provide the basis for interaction between political activity and the great themes of the Bible which will call into question all programmes and manifestos. The Christian in the political world badly needs this continual corrective, which will enable reflection on the experience of political activity and refine both actions and ideas. To borrow from liberation theology, what is at work is a 'hermeneutical circle'. The Christian is involved in politics. He/she reflects on that and raises questions/suspicions about what is going on, leading to a questioning of ideology. The Bible is brought to bear on those questions, and acts as a tool for understanding reality in the light of God's kingdom. That understanding leads to analysis, and back into action, upon which we again reflect. There are varieties of description of this 'hermeneutical circle', but that is perhaps its simplest expression.

Given a theological framework, the questions of *how* we operate are not entirely solved. There are several biblical ideas which, it seems to me, form the particular points of divergence between Christians in the realm of politics. They are—the doctrine of the fall, the relationship of the church and the world, and our understanding of the church itself.

It is our view of sin and the fall which conditions the way in which we see the potential of humanity in society. Peter Hinchliff puts it starkly. 'I believe that Christians really choose between capitalism and socialism on the basis of their often unconscious understanding of the fallenness of man.'[8] The capitalist will argue that the competitive market economy best harnesses the instincts and desires of fallen humanity for the good of all. The socialist will argue that the right ordering of society depends upon controlling unfettered competitive avarice for the good of society as a whole. Our view of the fall also conditions our estimate of how far society is capable of regeneration. If we see in the fall the concept that each person is as corrupted as they possibly could be, our view of what is achievable will be thoroughly pessimistic. If, on the other hand, we believe in the innate goodness of all, we will espouse a somewhat naive optimism about what is attainable. In point of fact, of course, the biblical view is between these two polarities—that human beings are still in God's image, though marred by sin. How we proceed from there is one of the points of divergence!

It is helpful, secondly, to give some thought to one's understanding of the church and its relationship to the world. Many people's models of social involvement stem from their particular view of the way in which the church as Christian community interacts with and is defined over against the world. Graham Dow charts this helpfully.[9] He talks of a variety of strategies—a Christian society, a Christian alternative, a Christian withdrawal, and a Christian leavening. The options for Christians are respectively to take over and govern society; to build an alternative society; to withdraw from society because the world is evil; or to seek to leaven society by involvement within it. Those who see the world as evil will want to work within the alternative/withdrawal framework, while those who see it as fallen but redeemable will learn the lessons of the past and the horrors of contemporary Ulster and South Africa, reject the idea of a Christian takeover of society as unwise and impractical, and work with some version of the 'leavening' model. But what *sort* of leavening?

Here again there is a clear divergence. Some would wish to keep the world/church divide very clear. Using the Augustine/Luther idea of two kingdoms—the kingdom of God and the kingdom of man—they would see the Christian's role as seeking to change and influence the world's political structures while operating in two separate realms. The problem with this is that it begins to pose a different standard and code of behaviour in each realm—rather as if one were playing two games with two sets of rules. *But God's world is one world, and the Christian cannot live with integrity as a kind of spiritual schizophrenic.* Alternatively, others committed to the 'leavening' idea would want to develop a model of action in which Christian activity and the mission of God are expressed in every place, and the world/church distinction becomes much more blurred. The shortcoming of this approach is that it becomes easy to submerge the distinctively Christian emphasis of one's activity.

Finally, the understanding of the church itself is crucial. The often-heard statement 'the church shouldn't get involved in politics' raises questions about what perception of the church underlies it. Hinchliff isolates four possible meanings.[10] First, there is *the ideal church*, the Bride of Christ (Eph 5:26–27), which is to be kept unsullied by the world. Secondly, there is *the local congregation*, the church of which you or I are members. Thirdly, there is *the denomination* to which we belong. Finally, and incorrectly, there is *the clergy/ leadership* of the church (as in 'John's going into the church', meaning 'he's going to be ordained').

These distinctions are helpful in clarifying what we actually mean by 'the church shouldn't get involved in politics'. Clearly, the ideal church, the Bride of Christ, is not a political entity, even though it partakes of the nature of the kingdom of God. If what people mean is that there is a high destiny for the church which transcends the human and temporal world of politics, then it is true to say that 'the church shouldn't get involved'. It is not necessarily true of the third and second definitions. Both the denomination and the local congregation are imperfect expressions of the ideal church, and are already part of the structures of society by virtue of their existence. There may well be circumstances where they will be forced into the political arena, or they may choose so to be involved. Obviously it is opting for politics which I am advocating.

The church *cannot* keep out of politics without neglecting its true role. It is a truism of history that it is dangerous for a church to be closely aligned with one particular government or political party. But there will be occasions when the church will wish, as denomination, to advocate a particular policy as being just or fair (such as the allocation of more money to urban priority areas); to criticize a policy as being unjust (for example, the British Nationality Act); or to raise questions over the conduct of public policy (as for example Bishop Bell did with regard to the saturation bombing of German cities during the Second World War). Recent debates in the Church of England over nuclear weapons have enabled the church to explore its role as conscience to the nation in seeking to define what limits there might be to the possession and use of such weapons.

The realm of politics will similarly impinge on the local

church at all levels, if the local church is willing to let it do so. For example, opposition to a road scheme, uniting to protest against the closure of a local school, or making representations to the local police about the methods they use when dealing with young blacks have all been on the agenda of churches known to me. Such issues require corporate action in order to explore them fully, and tackling them flows naturally from the church seeing itself as a place for caring compassionate mission. The fourth definition asks whether a Christian minister should be involved in political life. Considerations of time weigh heavily here. So does the fear that if a minister is identified too closely with a political party, he or she will be unable to minister acceptably to those not of his/her political persuasion. My own experience is that it is possible to minister to the whole community while being a member of a political party. A useful parallel is that of the elected councillor or M.P., who, though only elected by those supporting his or her party, has to represent and deal with the problems of the whole of his or her constituency. There is a distinction to be drawn here between the abuse of one's God-given role as teacher and pastor by using the pulpit for political purposes (illegitimate), and the capacity of the minister to exercise a political role in the community as part of his or her overall ministry.

Finally, what practical considerations are there for the Christian considering the call to politics? One immediate fear seems to be what is seen as the 'problem' of party politics. Christians will want to insist that no political party clearly encapsulates the totality of Christian truth. Yet it is the case that it is virtually impossible in contemporary Britain to have a significant role in local or national politics without joining a political party. Those who believe that their role should only be in the community may manage not to align. If, however, one wishes to exercise political responsibility as M.P. or Councillor, or to influence others in those roles, then membership of one of the four main parties is inevitable. No Christian of integrity is likely to agree with every policy espoused by a particular party, and part of the role of the

Christian in respect of party politics is to be able to say the unsayable and to criticize and question party shibboleths although this will sometimes be unpopular and difficult.

Party involvement is a matter for individuals. But should politics be a matter just for the individual, or for the whole church? I want to say that it is neither. It is a role for the church as community. Each church will possess within its ranks those whose gift and calling is to politics, and who already are, or ought to be, active in the community, their party, or Trade Union. The church needs deliberately to create cells of people to support them, pray and reflect with them, to be involved, as appropriate, in their ventures, to give them encouragement, and where necessary, to provide them with correctives to their thinking.

The whole church should be concerned to pray for them and to support them. There should be a willingness on the part of the PCC to make space on its agenda for items which emerge from their involvement, which become the concern of the whole church. For example, a local councillor is opposed to development plans for a hypermarket on derelict land in the parish. The church will want to be involved in the consultation process (if there is one), and will want those of its members involved in the local tenants' association, pressing for a community hall to be built, to get involved for lobbying for that particular concern. Thus the individual's isolated concerns are shared and become the property of the whole community. The vision we should be pursuing is one where politics is *always* on the agenda of the church, and where it becomes as natural as breathing to pray and discuss with our community workers, tenant leaders, councillors and M.P.s. Or perhaps one should say 'as natural as discussing worship, fabric and finance'?

All that I have written so far can relate to any Christian in any denomination. But this is a book on hope for the Church of England. Of course, social and political action should not just be the prerogative of the Church of England. The ecumenical principle 'never do anything separately which could be done together' applies particularly in the context of being involved in collective Christian political activity. None the less, the fact that the Church of England is the national church gives it a particular role in social action. First, because it is perceived by society as still having some significance, however marginal, in the life of society. At a local level, civic services, church schools, or the church's part in community consultation are examples of points of interaction between churches and political structures. Secondly, because of the parochial system, the Church of England sees itself as being responsible for a particular geographical area, and the people and the institutions within that area. Thirdly, because of the relationship between church and state, the church has a legitimate input into the political life of the nation (though whether the House of Lords is the most appropriate structure through which that input should occur is a wider question!).

In all this I am not defending the status of the Church of England as an established church. It is perfectly possible to be the church of the nation without having the monarch as head of the church and being subject to the whims of Parliament! Victor de Waal has described this special role of the Church of England as being in 'critical solidarity' with the nation.[11] The church lives in the culture, ethos and structures of the nation. That it cannot avoid. But it adopts a positive attitude towards that culture, and stands in solidarity with it, in so far as it can. It will, however, always be a *critical* solidarity, whatever government is in power, because the church has a higher responsibility at the same time.

I have been arguing that involvement is inevitable because of the nature of the mission of the church. Clearly, many Christians in the evangelical Anglican tradition have not yet been seized by that inevitability. I have been polemical in trying to suggest that the Church of England *needs* political involvement in order to be a 'whole' church, that there is an evangelical theology which provides a framework for that involvement, and that the 'problems' of involvement are less difficult than they are often alleged to be. Many people are called to politics—it is their gift. It is a crying shame that many have to exercise that gift outside the context of the Christian fellowship, and with no reference to it, because the local church will not support them.

The world of politics will become increasingly complex over the coming years. The need to relate Christian faith to that world will become more and more crucial. The Church of England has a unique role in this regard. Whatever the government of the day or media critics of the church might wish to argue, the political imperative cannot be ducked. Rather we should hear the call of God's kingdom and respond gladly, knowing that in the end that kingdom is the only enduring political structure.

Useful further reading

John Gladwin, *God's People in God's World* (IVP, 1979).
Paul Marshall, *Thine is the Kingdom* (Marshalls, 1984).
Graham Dow, *The Local Church's Political Responsibility* (Grove Books, 1980).

PART THREE

The Workers

LEADING THE MISSION OF THE PEOPLE OF GOD

by

*George Carey**

'Why am I a man of hope in these critical times?' asked Cardinal Suenens, repeating the reporter's question. 'I am a man of hope not for human reasons nor from natural optimism, but because I believe that the Holy Spirit is at work in the church and in the world even where his name remains unheard. I am an optimist because I believe the Holy Spirit is the Spirit of creation. To those who welcome him he gives each day fresh freedom and a renewal of joy and hope'.[12]

I echo these words as I look at our church today. Yes, to some extent the Church of England is reaping the harvest of years of neglect, squandered resources, boring and joyless worship and its lack of an evangelistic strategy. It is all too easy to believe that the church is in decline when we see it marginalized and irrelevant to national life. But there is another side to the picture. In my travels I have clear evidence of churches coming alive; congregations growing; lives being changed and wonderful things happening. Yes, I am talking about Anglican churches! Indeed, most of our students at Trinity come from churches which are alive and buoyant. What, we may well ask, are the reasons behind such growth,

---

*Dr George Carey has spent most of his ministry in theological education and is presently Principal of Trinity College, Bristol. He served a curacy in Islington and was Vicar of St Nicholas, Durham for several years. He is a member of General Synod, has written several books, is a member of the ACCM council and makes Anglican–Roman Catholic relationships a special area for study. He is married to Eileen and they have four children.

which goes against the national picture? Are there any common features at the heart of renewal?

I believe that there are, and that one of the most important is the quality of leadership. Churches grow where there is effective and spiritual leadership; churches decline where leadership is impotent and lifeless. Jesus was aware of the crucial importance of leadership and deliberately trained a number of key men to carry on his ministry after his death and resurrection. 'He appointed twelve to be with him and to be sent out to preach' (Mk 3:14). They saw him at work, teaching, loving, touching and healing. They entered into his ministry and served their apprenticeship working with the 'Master Carpenter'. To the church's shame it has not noticed clearly enough the importance of this example. Jesus did not lock the disciples away within the cloistered walls of a college or monastery. He did not teach them in isolation from the needs of society—he took them with him into the sphere of battle. They learned 'on the job'.

In this chapter I wish to explore the task of ministry from my experience as a theological teacher in four of our colleges—as well as being an incumbent of a church which had to face up to change. I hope that my remarks will be seen as a positive contribution to the debate about theological training. Where I criticize existing practices I trust that these comments will not be construed as negative and destructive, but remarks which emerge from a great concern that we should be more effective than we are already. Let me say without reservation that all the Anglican colleges are doing a fine work in training men and women for God's service today. The staff are highly dedicated, they work long hours and care passionately—as I do—about the quality of their work. The training we give today is far superior to that offered, say, twenty or even ten years ago.

What then, is wrong? If the training is so excellent, why don't we leave things as they are and let the colleges get on with their task of preparing people for ministry? There are many reasons why we cannot. We must leave to one side the sheer costs of maintaining expensive institutions. It is all too tempting for economic factors to dictate the future of theological education; nevertheless, at the very least the amount of money which is poured into training people for ordination should lead us to ask if we are getting value for money. There are, however, three more important issues to be faced which I believe to be far more crucial, which are:

(i) The *context* of training—the problem of taking people out of their culture and isolating them from a natural community by placing them in an artificial one.

(ii) The *relevance* of training—the tension between academic theological training and ministerial formation.

(iii) The *nature* of training—'pupil' v. 'disciple' models.

Let us introduce an imaginary couple to show the problem.

Pete and Paula are in their twenties and feel called of God to offer themselves to the rest of the body of Christ for full-time Ministry. Their PCC enthusiastically recommend them for ministry and eventually Pete and Paula are selected for training and end up in one of our colleges. Sadly they have to leave their supporting church where they have exercised an important ministry and move to another part of the country. No doubt they have three stimulating years in college and, hopefully, they go on to become an effective clergy couple somewhere. But if they are a normal couple the training may have caused three serious dislocations.

First, it may create a *cultural dislocation* by taking Pete and Paula from their cultural context and subtly changing them. Any form of training 'moulds' and 'forms', and we have to be very clear about what we are forming and whether we want to form in that particular way. For example, we have to acknowledge that Anglican training is middle class throughout and we have failed noticeably and lamentably in our attempt to train anybody for an effective working class ministry. By 'disculturizing' students we may end up making them less effective than they were. The recent report of the Archbishop's commission on Urban Priority Areas (ACUPA) makes this criticism very strongly:

In the Church of England ordinands coming from working class backgrounds become involved in an educational enterprise familiar to professional people but strange to their home environment, and are influenced by social expectations and patterns of behaviour which may distance them from their homes and neighbourhoods.[13]

Second, *ministry is dislocated* by the creation of a professional caste who are different from lay Christians because they know 'how to do' things. Without any question a form of mystique has formed around the ordained minister, leaving an unfortunate legacy in ill-equipped lay Christians unused to using their gifts in Christian service. It is not too sweeping to say that the majority of priests and ministers today (in whatever denomination we are talking about) *do not know how to give ministry back to the congregation.* 'Every-member ministry' is not a modern discovery—it is a mark of New Testament Christianity. It is regrettable that training for the professional ordained ministry has restricted the gifts of the people of God.

There is a third dislocation which is *functional* in character. We have removed the learner from the context of ministry; so 'ministry to' is replaced by 'ministry about' (the sick, the dying, the unchurched, etc.). I mean by this that instead of the 'disciple' practising ministry the 'student', or 'pupil', is taught it, mainly within the classroom situation, with insufficient time given to what we now call 'praxis'.

Thus the thrust of modern training is dominated by a model of ministry which is academic, information-centred, subject-oriented, professional, isolated and middle class. Now without pretending to have all the answers, I believe that it is possible to make some immediate and somewhat modest changes which will have a dynamic effect upon the church; and to these proposals I now turn.

Trainers should be gifted men and women of proven ability

I have no wish to impugn the staffs of our colleges because they are all gifted and committed people, selected by College Councils because they have specialist skills. But in the majority of cases these gifts are academic. So, for example, a college has need of a doctrine teacher and these days, thirty or forty able people will apply, many of whom have Ph.D.s in a relevant discipline. While, of course, other factors are constantly kept in mind—such as pastoral ability, commitment to the gospel, and so on—in the majority of cases the academic ability of a candidate is the key factor in appointments.

Now, if our concern is academic theology and if the acquisition of a degree is the all-important consideration, then clearly, we must appoint people of academic excellence. But if we are training people for ministry; if our concern is that people should leave colleges to 'lead the mission of the people of God', then other factors become much more important. I want to say plainly from my experience of ministry, that what the church needs are students who love their Lord, who have been called to his service, and who come with gifts to be sharpened and honed for the glory of God. And what they need are teachers who have been *proven* in battle; men and women who have been through the fires of ministry and can share that with those they teach.

I am not for one minute saying that theology is unimportant and that getting qualifications is valueless. There will always be a need on the staff of colleges for some who will see their ministries in terms of long-term service. Professionalism is very important, and I with many others am delighted that evangelical scholarship has grown over the last twenty years so that we are more able to play our part in the intellectual life of our church. But it has struck me as very odd and worrying that comparatively few on our college faculties have had incumbency experience or equivalent service in Christian ministry.

If we wish to get the proper balance between academic theology and ministerial training, we must as a matter of urgency ensure that half or even more of our staffs are people whose 'giftedness' lies in ministerial functions; who have been 'anointed' by God; and who have had some measure of 'success' in parochial ministry. This kind of reform will have an immediate effect, I believe, in the relevance of our theological training. The report *Faith in The City* (ACUPA), again, is very critical of the relevance of present styles of training: 'There are thousands of clergy today whose book-shelves as much as their styles of ministry are clear evidence that their theological training has borne little fruit in their life's work.'[14] Admittedly, this suggests that curriculum changes are essential but of greater importance, I believe, is the need to have theological staff whose vision of training is shaped by their own encounter with the living God in the cut and thrust of active ministry.

But, goes the objection, such people may be acceptable to teach ministerial skills but they are unlikely to be able to teach such specialist subjects as New Testament, Liturgy, Church History and so on. Have we not got to reckon with the fact that theology has become such a recondite subject that it is essential that those who teach must have the qualifications that go with the specialisms concerned, and that this means accepting the fact that they will be short on ministerial experience?

That conclusion only follows if we assume that we must continue the present form of doing things. I have pleaded elsewhere[15] for a more holistic approach to ministerial formation. We are still too 'subject' dominated in our attitude to learning—we dole out information on undigested topics like the authorship of Jeremiah, the Wellhausen hypothesis, Enhypostasis, Luther's *justus et peccator* concept; and students get progressively fatter files and more and more bewildered. It is possible to devise a system of teaching in most, if not all, of the subjects which emerge not from the arcane concerns of academic and intellectual enquiry but from the proper concerns of ministerial formation. Such a way of proceeding will not be less thorough or less intellectually demanding than the former way, but it will be seen to be more relevant to the purposes of training people for the ministry. The Danish philosopher, Kierkegaard, once remarked of Hegel: 'I asked him for a map of Stockholm and he gave me a map of Europe' meaning that Hegel's view of humanity lacked relevance and application. I think that a great deal of current theological thinking and training stands under that judgement also.

What we need, surely, are teachers who can offer the specific 'maps' as well as the broad and detached perspective. I know that there are many very able men and women with a proven track-record in Christian ministry who would make effective teachers. They have the intellectual equipment but they would be barred from most teaching jobs at the moment because our concentration is upon academic information and not ministerial formation. I get very sad and angry with the system when students say to us on return from their five-week summer parish placement: 'I was getting very dry spiritually in college, and it was wonderful to go into X's parish and see what God was doing. I must guard against the danger of becoming spiritually dry again this year.'

Somehow I just cannot imagine a disciple of Jesus saying that kind of thing on returning from ministry in Galilee!

Our emphasis should be on formation rather than information

You don't have to be an advanced student of the New Testament to see the principle of 'following' that marks discipleship. Jesus gathered men and women around him. His way of living became their pattern; he taught them to pray his way saying 'Our Father'; his way of service became theirs, and he even modelled it by washing their feet. Above all, they imbibed a concept of God as Heavenly Father which transformed their understandings of his nature. Jesus' Father was a God who acted, who worked in the lives of people, who answered prayer, who did miraculous things. Following the resurrection his disciples carried on Jesus' pattern. The first converts were formed by a four-fold diet of apostolic teaching, fellowship, prayers and community living (Acts 2:42). The earliest pattern of Christian nurture appears to have been the close modelling of teacher to disciple. So Priscilla and Aquila take the fledgling Apollos under their wing and teach him the 'way' more accurately (Acts 18:42). Paul himself underscores the importance of spiritual formation with his emphasis upon 'be imitators of me' (Phil 3:17) because he realized that the older Christian had a duty to form the beginner after the likeness of Christ. In a vivid image in Galatians 4:19 he pictured himself in birth desiring Christ to be formed in his readers.

As I see it, theological colleges could become a great deal more effective if we took this aspect of formation more seriously than we do at present. Let me try to work this out briefly. I would hope that any institution training people for ministry would have as its main ambition that of being a school of the Holy Spirit in which all in-training would deepen people's experience of God in every respect. I would hope that their prayer lives would grow. I would hope that direct encouragement was given, not only to learning more about the tools of prayer—contemplation, meditation, quietness and so on—but that students would have the time and space to explore the richness of a living relationship with Almighty God. I would also hope that encouragement would be given for people to share their spiritual lives with others by having a spiritual director so that they learn to open up to others, to acknowledge failure as well as success and weakness as well as strength. Such a community would be a worshipping community, centred upon the Eucharist or Holy Communion and learning all the skills that go toward leading worship with sensitivity.

Because the Renewal movement is an important strand in my own spiritual development I have no hesitation in saying that my concept of theological training would include an openness to all the insights God is bringing through Renewal to his people today. As well as helping students to be fine preachers and leaders I would hope we would help them to enter with confidence into ministries of healing and deliverance, and to have the knowledge to help others into deeper experiences of the Spirit and his gifts and graces.

I have, then, no hesitation in saying that spiritual formation is the most important education we could possibly give to our ordinands. Those who have a deep and continuing love for the Lord Christ are those who can cope with discouragement, apathy and all the demands of ministry. In Morris West's magnificent book *In the Shoes of the Fisherman* the Pope was asked what kind of men he was looking for. He simply replied: 'Those with fire in their hearts and wings on their feet'. That fire cannot be taught, but it is often caught in prayer or in a community open to all that God is doing.

I make no secret of the fact that the teacher who communicated this to me was Michael Green. Michael taught me the New Testament. He was a brilliant teacher but that was not the central thing which came across. What he communicated was not his knowledge of academic New Testament scholarship (although that was there) but his enthusiasm for Scripture and for the way it could become a life-transforming encounter with a holy God. And that enthusiasm flowed out of the classroom because it had first flowed into it. Michael's primary gift was, and still is, evangelism. His love for the gospel transformed our understanding of the Scriptures. But he did not leave his ministry in the classroom. He encouraged us to go out in mission and ministry with him on Pathfinder camps, on church missions and so on. We saw him at work, he witnessed our first fumbling attempts at speaking and leading others to Christ; and we grew by observing, doing, learning and doing yet again. This seems to me to be a clear New Testament pattern, and I would like to see this model becoming more central in our training.

Seminaries serving the church

We have already observed that there is a tendency for our theological colleges to be isolated from the rest of the church by two factors. The first is the predominating influence of academic theology taught by staff who, in the main, have not had direct experience of leading a congregation. The second isolating factor is that the context of 'school' has replaced that of 'church' in the making of the minister. It is encouraging to report that all colleges now take pastoral theology more seriously than they used to, and many, like my own college, make pastoral theology the central pivot of the curriculum and assess it as rigorously as any other subject. But that is not really good enough and critics can, and often do, point to some fundamental problems with our present way of teaching. First, they point out, classic theological education removes people from the arena of learning which is life experience itself. Second, by concentrating upon academic skills and performances many essential areas of ministerial function are neglected by the college. Among such we could easily identify:

Administration (filing, typewriting, office-management, etc.)

Counselling—marital particularly.

AVA skills in communication.

Personal family life and pressure upon one's home.

Leading a church forward and giving vision.

Supporting and encouraging the ministry of lay folk.

Importance of church architecture on worship and mission.[16]

Colleges, of course, are only too well aware that they cannot cover everything, and assume that the more practical aspects of ministerial formation will either be touched upon by the Pastoral department or covered adequately by training parishes. But Pastoral departments usually have so much to teach that many topics such as the above are dealt with very cursorily and most of us would be willing to admit that there are not many incumbents around who have all the gifts to cover adequately the areas mentioned above.

Quite clearly we must press for a closer liaison between church and college. One form this could take, following the Archbishop's report *Faith in the City,* is for at least one theological college to move lock, stock and barrel into a densely packed urban area, such as Liverpool, with the aim of engaging with ministerial training and formation in the context of pastoral need and social deprivation. This is surely not impossible as the bold move undertaken by St John's Nottingham from Northwood, London, in 1970 indicates. The strategy behind that move was to bring the college nearer to a university campus so as to enjoy the benefits of an academic environment. These days we are prompted by an equally important motive; namely, to integrate training with the real issues of our culture.

A less radical suggestion—and one that most colleges could adopt—is for the development of 'sandwich' training so that a student spends a substantial amount of time in a training parish and not just a mere five weeks as at present. Let us imagine Pete and Paula starting on their training which might take the following form:

Year 1. Foundational Theological Course: Two terms in which all basic units are covered as at present.

Year 1. Term 3. *Supervised Parish Placement:* A strictly monitored placement in a specially selected training situation in which parish and college unite in providing a context for learning which will raise essential questions concerning the nature of ministry today. Students might be put into teams of no more than five. Wives should accompany husbands, and those with children would do placements as close to college as possible.

Year 2. Term 4. Theological training continues in college and attempts made to link theological reflection with parish experience.

Year 2. Term 5. *Supervised specialist placement* which may be a choice of hospital, prison, counselling, welfare, education, evangelism, church growth, etc. Again this will be properly prepared and assessed leading to, say, a 5,000 or 10,000 word report.

Year 2. Term 6. *Parish placement,* which will extend a student's experience of the ordained ministry, perhaps concentrating upon public skills of preaching and teaching, occasional offices, leading meetings and so forth. Limited academic work will continue in this term and close co-operation between college and church is essential to make it work.

Year 3. A full year in college prior to ordination, which draws together the practical and theoretical aspects of the training programme. Because of the larger practical elements of the course, it should be easier for this final year to be a thorough exploration of the issues raised by pastoral training from biblical and theological viewpoints.

This is one possible model, suggesting that one year out of three is spent on the job in a training parish being closely supervised by an experienced minister who has been carefully prepared by the college, so that strict evaluation and monitoring is achieved. If, however, the House of Bishops, through its organ The Advisory Council for the Church's Ministry (ACCM) really believes that a three-year academic course is essential for under-thirty's, then it should not skimp on the costs involved in 'earthing' training for the ministry. It should be prepared to sponsor four-year courses as the Baptist Church does, and insist that one of the four is spent in supervised field education. An equivalent programme may be devised for the over-thirty-year-old student doing a two-year course—with, possibly, two terms being spent out in supervised field work.

Such is my concept of changes which could be put into effect with some ease and which, I believe, would revolutionize the state of the church's ministry. Of course far more radical training programmes could easily be presented, but this is one which could be implemented reasonably quickly if the church and colleges had the will to do so.

But what about our depleted colleges which, with such a scheme might be one-third empty while students were 'doing theology'? Such a situation would give the church the opportunity to grapple with an opportunity we have never taken up realistically—*in-service training*. Regular opportunities for clergy to return to the residential colleges for a term every three years for reading, recollection, study and spiritual refreshment, would be a marvellous boon for them—and, no doubt, indirectly for their congregations as well! Furthermore, with the extra places available, colleges could arrange short courses for 'ordinary' Christians who simply want to understand their faith better or communicate it more effectively.

Leaders of hope and vision

The Church of England is in ferment today and so are all the churches in this land. The ecclesiological map of this country is changing. Established, mainstream church life is declining and it is all too obvious that traditional forms of worship and church activity are no longer attractive to the majority of our contemporaries. Charismatic churches, however, are flourishing and, significantly, the House Church movement is growing numerically and in influence all the time. No longer can we sniff contemptuously at it because it is now a force to be reckoned with.

What I think God is saying is that it is time to put our own house in order, to return to a full-blooded gospel which demands total commitment and sacrifice. Many changes lie ahead for the Church of England. The soaring costs of maintaining ancient buildings will see many of them closing. The needs of people in our inner cities and on our crowded housing estates will surely call forth imaginative patterns of ministry to reach them. Maintenance policy must be replaced by mission, and a buildings mentality by a people-centred consciousness. The people of God must learn to travel light if they are to travel at all. And for all this we need leaders who are adaptable men and women of vision, open to change and to the Holy Spirit who is at work among us today, creating the church of tomorrow.

13

CHRISTIAN BELIEF AND THE TRAINING OF CHRISTIAN MINISTERS

by

*Ruth Etchells**

One of the good things that has emerged from the sharpening debate about what, as Christians, we believe, is the fresh recognition of our faith's apparent contradictions. We believe, for instance, in the effectiveness of Christ's dying for us: we also believe in the power of his rising again. We believe that he knew flesh. We also believe that he is and always was and always will be beyond flesh.

And often the most frustrating and timewasting arguments develop because a group of us has a new or fresh vision of one side of these oppositions, and asserts it ignoring or diminishing the other. 'Christ reigns from the cross' can be emphasized at the (unnecessary) expense of Christ taking his place in heaven, or Christ appearing to the startled disciples behind the locked doors of an upper room.

So the arguments about virgin birth and empty tomb have served to remind us of the importance of keeping our grasp on the 'both/and' nature of our Christian faith. And two of these that recent disputes have highlighted for us are crucial: for on

---

*Ruth Etchells is Principal of St John's College, Durham, which includes Cranmer Hall—a training college for ministry in the Church of England. She is the first woman to serve as the principal of a Church of England theological college. She was formerly Vice-Principal of Trevelyan College, Durham University and where she still lectures in both the English and Theology departments. She is a member of General Synod and has just joined the Doctrine Commission having formerly served on the Board of Education working party which produced the report *All are Called*. She describes herself as 'unrepentantly a member of the laity'.

our re-discovery of their richness there is real hope for the church.

The first of these is the 'both/and' of a gospel about this world, and a gospel about the world to come. In the light of recent work on Urban Priority Areas and the church, this re-discovery is crucial. That is, a re-discovery that to preach the kingdom is to say something both about *this* world, and about the eternal life *of which it is a part*. And this needs re-asserting. For in the battle for justice, liberty and compassion in society as aspects of the kingdom of God, the struggle is necessarily so material and its impact so immediate and physical, that it has been easy to lose sight of the fact that the social changes aimed at are not ends in themselves but aspects only of something much deeper. That even when every man sits under his own vine in peace and safety, as in certain golden decades in the world's history, and in certain biblical promises, *this* is not the kingdom of heaven: only a picture of it. Only a showing forth of one aspect of it.

And therefore the church is re-discovering what it means that 'helping mankind to heaven' and 'the struggle to social equality' are not alternatives, but aspects of each other. That the 'cure of souls which is both mine and thine' with which the Bishop charges the incumbent is for eternity as well as time, with consequences beyond this life and also in this life. Putting it simply: we are being reminded that 'heaven is our home' because Christ made it so: and that our calling as Christians is to work out what this means for now in the society in which we live, *and* for eternity in our corporate, our individual, our daily walk with God: and that these are two sides of the same calling, for what we do with our dailiness, whether socially or individually, is the very stuff of what we are making of our heaven-wardness.

Hence any vision of 'the kingdom' which is wholly based on or dependent on a buoyant economy or full employment or a welfare state, has transferred the emphasis dangerously: has made 'signs' of the kingdom *into the kingdom itself*. What I am urging is that because our faith is about the quality of this life *as part of eternity,* experiencing the kingdom is not in the end about my job or my house or my income. Grace, through Jesus Christ, and the knowledge and delight and freedom of grace, are not at the mercy of these, and we mislead men and women if we ever suggest that only employment and home ownership make God's grace possible. But conversely, the kingdom *is* about my responsibility as a Christian to struggle in the name of Heaven for social conditions for men and women which acknowledge their dignity and beauty as children of their heavenly Father. Squalid social conditions can never evacuate or dissolve grace; but *my* acquiescence in these conditions *for others,* can, and often does, hinder its operation. Yet at the same time, if my struggle for a 'better quality of life' for others is understood *only* in terms of 'this-worldly' good, then I have diminished the gospel and diverted its power. For its power is humanity's eternal good, not merely its temporal condition. And if it is ever proclaimed only in terms of the temporal, we have the cross without the transforming resurrection. If it is proclaimed only in terms of the eternal, of course, we have resurrection without the reality of the cross. *Neither* is closer than the other to the gospel: *we must have both.*

One of the reasons why we have found it so difficult to hold firmly to both sides of this opposition (grace in time, grace in eternity) and its absolute necessity to our salvation, is because we have tended to lose sight of another opposition, another 'contradictory pairing', in the Christian faith, which time and eternity are all about. That is, that God is a God of mercy, and also of justice, of justice and also of mercy. That his relationship with his creation is one of both judging and of reconciling; of reconciling and judging. And that just as, in the 'both/and' of time and eternity, eternity includes time, so in *this* 'both/and' 'reconciling' includes 'judging'.

The church's fresh recovery of this is comparable with re-establishing the second intersecting set of girders on which it stands firm. If we think of time and eternity as a continuous line in which time is included in eternity, and then we think of God's dealings with humankind as another continuous line in which reconciling includes judging; and we then note how the second line interacts with the first; we have a picture of that which the church is freshly recovering as its foundation of belief.

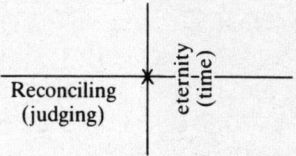

'X' marks the spot, the present moment, in society, and the individual heart, where God's dealing with us cuts across the time/eternity line and confronts us.

Before we go on to look at what is our present hope in the church in this re-discovering of the God who both judges and forgives, and what are some of the consequences, there is one more thing we must notice about the fresh insistence that we consciously live our lives daily in eternity as well as in time. That is, that the church daily recalls in its Holy Communion Service that moment in time in which most significantly and to eternal and unchangeable consequence, God's dealings with humanity cut across the time/eternity line and were visible in a present moment. And so, when we say that 'X marks the spot', the *present moment* in society and the heart where God's dealing with us confronts us *now*, we include in that 'now' that 're-call' of the moment in time when

God was man in Palestine
And lives again in bread and wine.

The recovery in our belief, of a fuller sense of the God who judges, as well as the God who is merciful to us, is a necessary return of binocular vision to eyes that have been in danger of squinting: or, at the very least, seeing one-eyed. For we have been very clear in the last fifty years—and the Archbishop's Commission on Urban Priority Areas has made it even clearer—that God is Judge of our society. There has been a real spirit of prophecy in the church, in the Old Testament sense of declaring the righteousness of God as a measure of the unrighteousness of society. Corporately we acknowledge judgement. We are, however, in the social area singularly lacking in the other half of the equation, and I have heard little said about God having mercy on, and reconciling to himself, those sinners seen as responsible for the unjust state of society. He is, instead, understood as a God of mercy to the victims of society only.

The hard message for popular social theologians is that he is a God of mercy to all alike, the sinners of oppression as well as the sinners of depression. '*All* have sinned, and fall short of the glory of God.'

There is a consistent tendency to claim his mercy (and not his judgement) on behalf of the poor, and his judgement only, and not his mercy, on the comparatively affluent. *The power of the gospel is that it addresses each:* each and all: and we diminish it and corrupt it if we preach one gospel for the poor and another for the non-poor. It is like preaching grace for murderers but not for rapists. Its *consequences* are totally different for the two groups: though let us rid ourselves of the romantic notion that the poor in society are sinless, and the comfortable in society are the sinful. '*All* have sinned, and fall short of the glory of God'. All—rich and poor alike—are called to penitence, individual and social: all are called to his reconciliation. *And that means reconciliation with each other as well as with God.* I cannot think of a more corrupting and divisive gospel than that which sees, one-eyed, God's judging and mercy, and apportions it to separate groups, judgement to one group, mercy to the other.

God is not biased: by definition he cannot be biased. His judgement is of all: his mercy is for all: his reconciling humankind to himself is of all humanity, through all time and all space. Zaccheus the wealthy and Saul the socially upper-class are called and forgiven as much as the down-trodden Peter: bourgeois boat-owners Simon and Andrew are called as well as the destitute. The effect of this, in calling forth a proper response from different groups, will differ sharply: knowing God's judgement on one's comfortable state in society, and his mercy on one's sinfulness in that position, calls out an utterly different *kind* of penitence and action from that to which one is moved in a state of penury and deprivation. But whichever one's state, God's judgement *and mercy* alike addresses. And it is the worst kind of deprivation to deny the reality of his judgement to the poor and the reality of his mercy to the non-poor. The profound truth of the parable of Dives and Lazarus is that God's grace is for both: the profound horror is that only one of them accepted it: and the Christian 'type' of it is that Lazarus would be praying for *Dives'* salvation as much as Dives is required to further Lazarus' good.

There is a second form of 'squint' we have been suffering from in the past, which this re-discovery of the 'both/and' of judgement and mercy helps to put right. That is: we have applied 'judgement' almost exclusively to the affairs of this world and almost exclusively we have applied 'mercy' to the things of eternity. 'Judgement' as a condition of eternity is not something we have been accepting of: we have applied too easy a mercy, too facile a resurrection, to our eternal destiny. And this not only has its effect in diluting the power and force of the gospel in the journey in eternity of each individual soul: it also has its effect on the gospel we preach to society. For if, as Scripture and our life with him makes clear, our life in society *now* is part of eternity, then we are transacting heaven's business now, and therefore our society stands under *eternal* judgement, not merely temporal.

So the church's hope for today lies in re-discovering the time dimensions of the gospel. 'Eternity' only takes on meaning if we believe that it is the real condition of humanity, and that God's judging takes place in *that* dimension as well as in our social 'today'. 'Judgement' only takes on its full power if we recognize afresh that it is the real situation of humanity before God, and that it applies equally to this world and *the next*. Our rebellious society, our rebellious church, and our rebellious individual human hearts, have come close to glossing over, hiding from ourselves as unacceptable, the unchanging truth of 'judgement' and 'eternity'. And so, of course, the gospel is diminished: for what need of God's extraordinary and mind-boggling grace in 'reconciling the world to himself' if the church, let alone the world, has little sense of any need of such eternal reconciling? The movement, therefore, to recover the 'both/and' of judgement and mercy as we stand before Heaven's judgement throne in the eternal places, is almost the greatest movement of hope I discern in the church today.

For God's 'judgement' of us declares us to be of value, to be worth making a judgement about: it restores the 'infinite' to our sense of the nature of our souls: it reminds us that human-kind is mortal and immortal: that our *destinies* are not finite: that our actions and our very state of being have infinite, not merely finite, consequences. That heaven is our home: and that the work of Christ is to recover it for us.

I have said that today's hope in the church lies in its steady recovery of these contradictory truths of its belief, and its applying them in the dailiness that is our eternity. For me that has a sharply relevant particularity. For part of my job is to be Principal of one of the Church of England's theological colleges, training men and women for full time ministry in the church. What does recovering the 'both/and' of time and eternity, justice and mercy, say to the training of our ministers?

First, that the context and *content* of that training must reinforce the fact that the gospel is about both this world and the next, about now and about eternity. In plain terms, what are the implications of this?

The place where training happens

1. The place where training happens, and the form of training, must give equal weight to both. This means that any training which wholly or largely withdraws the student from the world, from the 'now' of our faith; and any training which wholly or largely immerses the student in the world, with no time or space to reflect on the 'for ever' of our faith, are perhaps equally imbalanced theologically.

2. The implications of this are clear. I cannot see a proper theological basis for wholly or largely residential training:

neither can I see a proper basis for wholly or largely non-residential training. We have to reform the present style of training, both in residential colleges and non-residential houses, causing them to converge, if we are to be true to our re-discovery of the 'both/and' of our Christian belief. Quite apart from educational grounds and sociological grounds, the theological basis of training and its proper spirituality demands that the student spends part of his or her training 'out there' in the undefended world: and an *equal* part (but only an equal part) in withdrawal (as Christ did to desert, or mountain) in reflection and feeding, at God's hand, to ponder the nature of judgement and mercy as experienced alike in the 'Thus says the Lord' to society for today, and 'Thus says the Lord', for ever, to the human heart. Only so is ministerial *formation* possible.

3. It follows that the rough division between 'residential' training for full-time ministry and 'non-residential' training for non-stipendiary, should disappear.

4. It follows that no training should be fully residential: but that a flexible pattern of training should be developed. There could be, for instance, one or two or three years' residence with two years' first curacy between them (a sort of 'sandwich' course): or one year's residence followed by two or three years' part-time training, in which the student has systematized experience of the world 'out there' under supervision from vicar and college; or of two years' part-time training at the theological training centre nearest to the student's own home, followed by a residential year somewhere quite different: the possibilities are endless. What is clear is that *theologically* the present pattern really isn't very satisfactory.

The consequences of training

1. There are consequences for the training curricula as well. The student needs to develop a sense of the God of history who from beyond history and beyond the future has acted in a moment of time: the student also needs to relate this to how God is addressing this present moment and this present

society and the 'now' of individual human beings. So there remains a need for training in the history of God's dealing with the world and the church and with individuals: but the emphasis needs to be on the *theology* of this, the 'what God was/or is doing' aspect of it. The student's own growth in understanding of God's ways with men is the point, not the amassing of information. And if this is to be connected up in the student's imagination with today, and God in action today, and the nature of God's judgement and mercy today, then past, future and present, eternity and now, this world and the next, need gathering together in the student's learning and thinking under aspects of God's dealings with human-kind, aspects of God's nature, rather than sequentially or chronologically, labelled 'History' or 'Sociology' or 'New Testament' or 'Old Testament' or 'Systematics'. I have become more and more sure that at the heart of our curricula, whether in the 'world' centred practical training or 'spirit' centred development training, or in the 'mind' centred academic training, we need to be dwelling on the *nature of God* in his dealings with creation.

2. It follows that 'spirituality'—the daily living with and listening to and reflecting on God at work in the world and the human heart—should be the formative and connecting and shaping link between all the aspects of a student's training for ministry. For in the end the task of the student is to help souls heavenward and challenge the society that hinders the journey: and the student who is not growing *through* training into a profounder awareness of the nature of God's judge-ment and mercy, and the fact of 'now' being part of eternity and eternity being expressed in the dailiness of 'now', is not properly preparing for Christian ministry.

The reality that comes from training

1. There is one other obvious consequence of this re-discovery of the 'both/and' of our belief, for the training of Christian ministry. That is, that the reality of being 'under judgement' needs to become part of the student's emotional,

and spiritual equipment: it needs to become part of the student's very personhood. Otherwise mercy and reconciling—'grace'—have no force in the life of that student:

> How are men to call upon him in whom they have not believed? And how are they to believe in him of whom they have never heard? And how are they to hear without a preacher? (Rom 10:14, RSV)

2. How shall the reality of our God as one dealing with us in both judgement and mercy, subsuming both in reconciling us to himself, be preached if our ministerial students are not themselves fully seized of it?

What, again in plain terms, does this mean in training?

3. It means a recognition of the spirit of our age which runs counter to any acceptance of judgement imposed 'from without'. This is perceivable in the way society's structures resist the voice of Christian admonition: it is *equally* apparent in the refusal of individuals to accept responsibility *as* individuals for their own sinfulness, blaming it instead on structural oppression.

4. It therefore follows that students need to be trained in recognizing the force of this in their own assumptions and attitudes, and helped to grasp wholeheartedly that the spiritual reality of this life and the next involves accepting that judgement from without which is most profoundly merciful and healing, the judgement of God.

5. And in order to assist this the habit of self-judgement, self-assessment, personal, spiritual, pastoral and academic must be built into the training: but a self-assessment which is founded on a reliance on God's reconciling, and one which therefore soberly and hopefully sits under scrutiny. This again needs to be rooted in the nature of our Christian belief: which sees the material of every day as the matter of eternity, and alike under his judgement and mercy. Such capacity for self-criticism, far from being introspective, is rooted in a certainty of God's reconciling me to himself with this, even this, failure or bad practice or carelessness or laziness or selfishness or narrowness on my head. So neither pride of achievement nor self deprecation of failure have any place in this kind of self

assessment; only a realism about where I stand in my training as minister, and how God's grace contains me in it.

6. The whole process therefore of examinations and reports and final recommendations and the like, needs aligning to this 'both/and' nature of Christian belief.

That is how the contradictory nature of our Christian belief works out for me as I consider part of my job and where it ought to be developing. The context of training, the content of training and the nature of assessment need all alike to spring from this knowledge of a God who judges and reconciles, and whose address to us is for now and for ever, for the individual and for the whole of society. What gives me hope are the signs that this is being struggled with at this very time in the church. Christ reigns from the cross. He is Lord *also* of the empty tomb. God has judged in time and out of time: and reconciled to himself every student in training, for now and for eternity.

14

SHARED MINISTRY IN THE LOCAL CHURCH

by

*Mark Birchall**

There is hope for the Church of England, because so many positive factors in the area of shared ministry have suddenly begun to come together in the last ten years.

The growing acceptance that ministry is of great variety, and requires the active involvement of every member; the expectation of finding gifts within the congregation to match the variety of tasks; the desire to develop relevant worship, to use culturally appropriate music and language, to strengthen both the internal life of the body and its outgoing service to the community—all these are increasingly recognized as essential features of a growing church.

But there is more. It is also becoming more widely accepted that the traditional solitary clergyman working on his own cannot possibly bring this every-member ministry into being, and then develop and use it. He needs a team. A few big churches can afford a full-time team; but in the vast majority of places it must be a lay team—a pastoral team, a local eldership, a local ministry team—the title matters hardly at

---

*Mark Birchall retired early from a career in stockbroking to give his full time to Christian work. He has a wide range of interests and involvements including membership of the Council of Trustees of the Mayflower Family Centre, and serving on the Board of Christian Weekly Newspapers Ltd. He is a member of General Synod and serves on the Advisory Council for the Church's Ministry (ACCM). He has a special interest in lay training and shared local church leadership. He has visited and studied experiments in shared leadership in 165 churches. He is a Reader at his local parish church.

all. Some form of shared leadership is seen to be essential, if any church growth vision is to be translated into reality. Not only is this increasingly widely accepted as a theory; in many places it is beginning to be put into practice.

The development of shared leadership

A widely accepted vision

Long-established institutions are usually conservative by nature. The Church of England is such an institution.

It is therefore very remarkable indeed that the idea of shared leadership has made such progress in recent years, at every level in the church:
1. Church authorities, diocesan and national, are increasingly coming to recognize that some sharing of leadership at the local level is essential, if the whole people of God are to be mobilized for mission.
2. At the grass roots, an increasing number of parishes are in the early stages of developing various kinds of local lay pastoral leadership teams.
3. There has been an explosive increase in the opportunities for lay training, and in the number of people participating.

Why has this happened so suddenly?

Roland Allen was a lone voice arguing for indigenous leadership in the church, in the 1920s—and he forecast that it would be fifty years before his ideas were accepted! Since the early 1960s, there has been an increasing flow of books in this area,[17] starting with the 1960 and 1962 reprints of Roland Allen's own writings. We are now seeing their gradual cumulative effect, at every level in the church. Many of them have been widely read in the parishes; others are more specialized; but all point in the same direction.

Four other factors have contributed substantially. First, the Charismatic renewal movement of the last twenty-five years has helped open our eyes. Church leaders began to see the possibility of change and lay people realized that they might have gifts to offer. Secondly, statistical evidence has become increasingly available, from the Church Growth movement and elsewhere, showing that almost all growing churches have some form of plural leadership. Thirdly, there is the bandwagon effect. When people are seen to be excited about a new idea, others want to try it out too: 'St John's has an eldership scheme, so we must do the same . . .' This rapid spread of ideas has been facilitated by the distribution of tapes describing the experience of well-known churches, and also through 'celebration' type gatherings and conferences.

Finally, and most important, *it is seen to be no longer possible to claim direct New Testament authority for any particular denominational structure of ministry*. As a result people are looking not for precise blueprints but for guidelines. Both in the New Testament and in the church of the earliest post-apostolic generations, they are finding evidence of variety and development to meet local needs. But they are also finding one common thread through it all—the idea of plural leadership in the local church seems to be virtually universal.

All this is at last beginning to erode the effects of centuries of clericalism, which has so deeply identified the church (both in its own eyes, and in the eyes of the world around it) with the ordained ministry, and so in effect with the one ordained man in each parish. We now have a situation where statistical evidence, practical experience, popular and more scholarly writing, and sheer commonsense are all in very close accord with biblical foundations. There must indeed be hope for the church!

The perceived advantages of shared leadership

If we had not been so blinkered by tradition, common sense would have told us that the one-man ministry was a virtual guarantee of non-growth. We should not be surprised that 92% of the 35,499 Protestant churches in England have less than 150 attenders on an average Sunday—the maximum size that one man on his own can reasonably cope with[18]—and that the vast majority of those congregations were then either static in size or declining. Something more than a one-man leadership seems to be an essential pre-condition of growth. The obvious advantages of shared leadership include:

(i) *More pastoral care* A team can multiply pastoral care at every level, either by sharing in it themselves, or by enabling others to do it. With a developing pastoral team, it becomes possible to:

- ▶ provide more effective welcome for newcomers and nurture for beginners, and more thorough preparation for baptism and marriage as well as better follow-up.

- ▶ offer continuing pastoral care to all members, instead of only when there is a crisis; so helping both to build up every individual towards maturity, and to strengthen the common life of the body.

- ▶ develop the gifts of those already involved, either through wider participation in worship, drama, music and prayer; or in 'good neighbouring' and other local community activities; or in teaching and leadership of groups; thus channelling people's energy and enthusiasm into the most appropriate forms of training and service.

- ▶ understand the pressures faced by those with demanding secular jobs, and support them, or help them find support elsewhere, so that they can be more effective salt and light in the structures of society.

- ▶ sort out problems of relationships, including marriage and other family difficulties, and provide the necessary continuing care and appropriate help for others in need.

(ii) *More effective planning* Ideas, plans, and policies can be dealt with more effectively by a Church Council (and are likely to meet with readier acceptance!) if they are broached on the basis that they have been thought through thoroughly beforehand by a known and trusted team, and do not merely represent the current bee in the Vicar's bonnet! This applies equally to

▶ developments in worship

▶ plans for evangelism and neighbourhood care

▶ liaison with other local churches and community organizations.

As the body with legal authority, the Church Council is always free to reject or modify plans laid before it; but it is usually too large a body for effective preparation of policy and plans in these areas.

(iii) *More relevant teaching* A team can broaden the teaching ministry of the church—both in the pulpit and through house groups. With the team's varied secular experience, it ought to be easier to relate and apply the word of God (and the wisdom of previous generations) to the actual problems faced by members in today's rapidly changing world. Further, in many places the local team, because they know the local scene and are part of it, can help the incoming professional minister relate more effectively to local conditions.

(iv) *Easier discipline* On the occasions when some form of discipline or rebuke is necessary, it can be extremely difficult for one man on his own to face up to the need, to take action, and then still to retain a pastoral relationship with those involved. A team is more likely both to reach the right decision and to be able to implement it in the most sensitive way.

(v) *Reduced pressure on the clergy* The stress on clergy marriages and on their family life and personal health painfully underlines the pressures caused by the present state of affairs. Many dedicated clergy are already working too hard, and not coping adequately with what they know needs to be done; a few have given up trying.

(vi) *Foundations for growth* At present, few churches plan for growth, and few have the capacity to cope with growth if it should come. Shared leadership may not initially reduce the pressure on the clergy, but it is in fact the only way of providing this capacity. Where churches have grown dynamically, it is tempting to attribute their success to their 'super-star' clergy: it is interesting to note that without exception these leaders, however gifted themselves, are people who can draw out, develop and use the complementary gifts of others, so creating an effective leadership team.[19]

In the last ten years an increasing number of local churches have begun to move this way, all across the country, in almost every denomination, and in virtually every type of neighbourhood—inner city, urban, suburban, city-centre, market-town, commuter/rural, remote rural, and holiday/retirement areas.[20]

Frequently, the movement is hesitant, tentative, experimental; it takes a variety of forms, often depending as much on the size of the congregation as on the spiritual maturity and capacity of the potential lay leadership.

Shared leadership in smaller churches

The NIE Survey showed that in 1979 two-thirds of Anglican congregations had a membership of less than 100—or a usual Sunday attendance of less than 70–80 adults. In such parishes it is easy for the Vicar to meet regularly with a small group and increasingly to share his ministry with them. It may naturally be the churchwardens, and the Reader if there is one. It may be the Standing Committee of the Church Council. It may be the house group leaders, or those already involved to some degree in pastoral caring. In many small churches a handful of people may cover all these roles! The emphasis may at first be mainly on pastoral work, or on worship, or on policy and planning; but wherever it starts, sharing in any aspect of ministry usually leads people into a deeper sense of responsibility, and so towards greater maturity and a greater capacity to share in leadership. The group may be described as an extended staff meeting, or as a pastoral team, or as a local eldership—the name matters little. What matters is that it is beginning to make possible the better pastoral care, and the more effective planning, which are the foundations for growth.

Shared leadership in larger churches

At the other end of the scale, in the few [21] large churches with a membership of say 400 (or a usual Sunday attendance of over 300), there is often a full-time staff of three or more clergy. There may also be a part-time administrator or Director of Music; there are large teams of people involved in Sunday Schools and Youth work, and in visiting, all needing oversight and care. Some such churches have effectively expanded their staff meeting or Standing Committee into what could be called a Heads of Departments team; others have opted for a smaller and less formal 'think-tank' group to meet with the staff for strategic planning. Some have created a formal lay-eldership, usually with a pastoral emphasis. The larger the full-time staff, the more difficult it is to draw the lay leadership into a real sharing of responsibility, partly because of the pressure of time, and partly because the staff team is bound to meet more frequently than the wider group, thus developing a separate group identity.

Shared leadership in middle-sized churches

The majority of Anglican worshippers, however, belong to churches between these two extremes. It is here that the movement towards corporate leadership seems most common, but also most difficult to work out well, because of the pressure of time. The church is too big for a small team to be able to know everyone and to share responsibility for everything: but there often appears to be too few leaders to cover all that needs to be done without putting unacceptable pressure on those involved. It is therefore particularly important to work out what is most appropriate to the needs of the church and to the gifts available and to start there: to develop a pastoral team, or a house group leaders team, or a worship and teaching team, or an extended staff meeting to work on policy; and to accept that not everything *can* be shared in this way at first. It is here, however, that the development of real shared pastoral leadership is most vital. The majority of these churches have a vicar and at most one other staff member—usually a curate in his first post. Statistics show that such churches are self-limiting in numbers, unless there is an effective spreading of pastoral responsibility, away from the one man at the centre.

In all these situations, pressure of time on busy lay people, and the risk of overburdening a small team, will always be limiting factors. So is the shortage of people with the necessary experience or ability. There should be no shame or sense of failure in saying 'We are simply not ready for an eldership team of the kind we hear about, the kind we would love to have'. Too often, we are conditioned by our 'instant' world. We are not used to having to wait for what we want, particularly if we are convinced that what we want is essential for the furtherance of God's work. But patience is likely to be rewarded. Firstly, the ground always needs to be carefully prepared for any change. There is great advantage in moving slowly and gradually towards the ultimate objective: in doing what can be done with the people who are available and within the constraints of their existing commitments. But secondly, and more important, there is now the increasing availability of people with some experience of pastoral responsibility (perhaps through leading house groups) or with some form of adult Christian education, or training, as a result of the great variety of training schemes which have mushroomed in recent years. The resources of available skills are growing very rapidly indeed.

The growth of training initiatives

In the last ten years there has indeed been a dramatic increase in opportunities for training. Most dioceses, and many deaneries, now have regular or occasional lay training courses, often leading to some form of Bishop's Certificate. Schools or Institutes of Christian Studies have sprung into life. Para-church agencies like Scripture Union, Bible Society, Youth with a Mission, Navigators, the Church Pastoral Aid Society, and many others are training young Christians (and some not so young) on a scale undreamt of even ten years ago. There are local Ministry Training Schemes—some with lay people training alongside ordination candidates. The St Johns Nottingham Extension Studies course has 1,000 students. A record number of Readers are in training. Many large churches have set up their own lay training programmes in recent years; the mobility of the population ensures that this resource will become an increasing benefit to the whole church as the years go by, as those who have been trained in the key centres spread out more widely across the country. Archbishop William Temple's call for a 'massive explosion in training for the laity', made over forty years ago, is at last becoming a reality.

Four general points are worth making. First, a great deal of initiative has come from outside Anglican circles. Secondly, in the case of diocesan schemes, there seems often to have been little forward planning as to how those being trained were to be used. Thirdly, there is no single effective clearing house for information on what is going on in different places, so there is little scope for learning from successes or failures experienced elsewhere. Nonetheless, the combined result is a rapidly increasing pool of people who are beginning to be equipped to share in all forms of ministry, including the ministry of leadership in the local church. There is a long way to go, but a very remarkable start has been made.

Diocesan and deanery schemes

A number of dioceses now run evening-class type courses leading to some form of Bishop's Certificate. At least 11 are using a course based on material first developed for Salisbury Diocese in 1977, and one claims that 2,500 people have now obtained their certificate. On similar lines, Gloucester Diocese launched *Framework for Faith* in 1981 as an ecumenical two-year course, in local groups, for individuals wishing to explore basic Christian beliefs. About 190 people have already completed the course. The diocese has now started a second-stage, centrally run, *Framework for Service*. This offers units on lay participation in Worship, Counselling, Working with Groups, Prayer, Teaching children and working with young people. Like most diocesan schemes, there is no advance commitment by the individual to their parish to use what they learn, nor vice versa.

By contrast Wakefield Diocese, whose Shared Ministry Project also began in 1981, has from the start asked parishes to formally call and send members onto their course, and to give an assurance to use them when they have completed the course. There is no certificate, but an appropriate form of local commissioning. The emphasis is on sharing with the incumbent in particular aspects of local ministry. Following a pilot scheme in one deanery centre in 1981–2, it expanded to four centres in 1982–3 and six in 1983–4. So far, 341 people have completed the course, and it is now running in six centres with a further 100 participants. At the same time, a good number of previous students have come back for a variety of further sessions, on counselling and other aspects of pastoral work. A survey in 1984 indicated that 80% of past students were then being effectively used in their parishes.

In Southwark Diocese, one deanery set up a course in 1976, on a basis similar to Wakefield's. It has run in alternate years, and over 100 people have completed it, with another twenty-two on the present course. It offers an introduction to basic doctrine, church life, pastoral care and community needs. About half the past students are still actively involved in some form of shared ministry; some doing what they were doing previously but with extra knowledge or confidence, as a result of the course, while others have taken on new responsibilities.

At a more professional level, the East Midlands Ministerial Training Course, the St Albans Ministerial Training Scheme, the Gloucester School of Ministry, and to a lesser extent other part-time courses recognized by the Bishops for ordination training, are also training a number of lay people who do not feel called to ordination or to accredited lay ministry. There are at present about 111 such lay people on these courses. Secondly, a number of dioceses are now in the early stages of developing training schemes for local ministry, where it is envisaged that individual members of the teams may in due course be called by the local church to a local ordained ministry, while others continue as lay ministers.

Several such schemes are at the planning stage; in a few dioceses, pilot courses are under way; Lincoln seems to have gone furthest along this road. The first twenty-seven students completed the three-year Lincoln scheme in February 1985, five of whom were then ordained to a local ministry. About 100 are in training, in fifteen groups across the diocese, in both urban and rural areas. Of these, a dozen are likely to be ordained, although this number is likely to increase once women can become deacons. Students are chosen to go on the course by their parishes, but the Diocese and the Advisory Council for the Churches Ministry share in the process of selection for ordination. Lincoln hope to develop a ministry team of up to a dozen people in each parish or group of parishes, led by one or more full-time clergy, and expect three or four within each local team to be called to local ordination. Since this new scheme began in 1982, they have also noticed increased numbers coming forward for training as Readers, or for traditional Non-Stipendiary Ministry.

Extension studies

Another exciting development is the Extension Studies course set up in 1977 by St John's College, Nottingham. This has rapidly built up to a total of about 1,000 students. Most of them are working towards a Certificate in Christian Studies, which requires completion of six units, out of eighteen possible courses in Biblical Studies, Doctrine, Ministry and Practical Theology. The training includes a summer school or similar residential element. It is run by two full time staff, with 120 local tutors all over the country. Fourteen Dioceses in the Anglican Communion have so far accepted the certificate as part or the whole of training required for individual readers, pastoral assistants, or other specialist lay ministry; six are using it in their training for Non-Stipendiary or local ordained ministry, and others are thinking of using it more widely in other local programmes. A growing number of 'extension' students are now working in groups, rather than on their own. A survey was recently undertaken of the first 140 who completed the course; of the eighty-three who replied:

▶ twenty were previously in some form of recognized

ministry (readers, local preachers, or full-time church workers) before taking the course.

► thirty are now in such ministry, or training for it.[22]

► eleven more are seriously considering such work, and

► ten of those who have become readers/local preachers are now considering going on to ordination or other full-time work.

Almost all the forty-one new prospective entrants into recognized ministry said that the course 'played a substantial part' in their decision. Current trends indicate that the number of those actually completing the course is steady, at about forty each year. A few drop out completely, while many either only set out to do the one or two units in which they are interested, or else find that pressure of time delays their completion of the full course. Nonetheless, this represents a very considerable extra resource of people at least partly equipped to share in local ministry, as well as a significant potential addition to the ranks of full-time and recognized ministry.

Schools and institutes of Christian studies

These too are all new in the last ten years. Some are entirely independent; most are ecumenical; some, like the Chiltern Christian Training Scheme[23] at High Wycombe, have strong links with their diocese, including a measure of financial support. There is no standard pattern. Some have a regular study programme, with evening-class courses lasting a year or longer, very like many of the Diocesan schemes; others lay on shorter courses or individual events in response to local needs. As in most of the diocesan schemes, the emphasis is usually more on adult education, rather than training for particular work, but this too can be a valuable part of the overall process. More lay people are being at least partly equipped to participate more actively as Christians in the church and the world.

Individual churches training activity

Many churches would probably claim always to have been involved in some form of lay training. Here too there has been significant progress in recent years. A handful of churches now have full-time Directors of Training (clerical and lay); others have someone doing this on a part-time basis. Some have recently started Adult Christian Education for everyone—often called the all-age Sunday School: like Extension Studies, this is common in other countries, especially in the USA, but still almost unknown here.

One long-established lay-training programme is at All Souls, Langham Place, London W1. This took a big step forward in 1977, since when about 120 members (one-quarter of them from other churches) have attended the Core Year course annually. As well as doctrinal studies, this includes an in-depth introduction to a specific area of work which people are expected to move into when their training finishes. The course requires one evening a week plus three to four hours homework, and two weekends a year: the course material is now being rewritten for publication, so that it can be used by churches which lack the staff resources of All Souls.

Another London church, St Helens, Bishopsgate, launched 'Read Mark Learn' in 1977. Three groups studied Mark's Gospel for a year; three leaders in each group were at the same time being trained to lead the group in their weekly study. There are now thirty-five groups, with 350 members, and eighty involved in learning how to lead groups at the same time as leading them. A second year has been added, to give a wider biblical perspective. Here too preparations are under way for introducing the system to other churches.

With the increased availability of distance learning material, including video, from Scripture Union, Church Pastoral-Aid Society, and elsewhere, there are now first class aids available for churches to run their own training programmes. Administry[24] estimate that one quarter of their 150 member churches are now using video training and educational material on a regular basis; and more and better material is becoming available all the time.

Para-church agencies

So much new work has begun, or expanded dramatically, in the last ten years that it is only possible to refer briefly to a few individual developments. In 1978 the Bible Society ran three short courses on Church Growth. Since then they have held another 236 courses (usually on a Friday evening and all day Saturday) attended by over 17,000 ministers and lay leaders from over 5,200 churches. Research in 1983 indicated that in at least half these churches decline has been arrested or new growth had begun. Meanwhile, the practical and positive thinking promoted by church growth teaching (maturity, as well as numbers) has become widely accepted, at least in theory; and in 1985 the Society recruited nine Associate Tutors to help meet steadily rising demand for this course. Scripture Union, by contrast, is no newcomer to the training scheme. Since the training staff was separated from their Education work in 1980, it has grown from four to six full-timers while associate trainers have risen from ten to sixty. SU estimates that it is now providing some form of training in evangelism, pastoral care, or work with children for between ten and fifteen thousand people every year. SU are also pro-ducing packaged training material for local church use in counselling, and in small group leadership, to add to their established material for children's work. In 1982 SU started small courses to assist lay leaders in local churches in training their own teams—particularly for co-ordinators of house groups, and leaders of pastoral visiting teams.

Very large numbers have also received valuable training as part of the preparation for Mission England and Mission to London meetings in 1984 and 1985. In total, over 80,000 attended Christian Life and Witness Classes, and 20,000 the course for prospective nurture group leaders. Over 30,000 served as counsellors. The material for these classes has been carefully revised and adapted to suit the British market. Many local churches reported immense benefit to their continuing programmes, as a result of this extra training and experience.

Bible Society, Scripture Union, and Mission England all estimate that about 40% of their participating churches are Anglican.

Youth and student work

Some organizations are seeing explosive growth in their training for youth work. The Church Pastoral-Aid Society now has 800 groups in CYFA (Church Youth Fellowships Association), growing at about 100 groups a year; 340 attended their leaders conference in 1983, and 700 in 1985. The same is true across the age-range; their 1400 Pathfinder groups are growing at more than 100 a year, and numbers attending regional leaders training conferences have also doubled in the last few years. There seems to be an increasing appetite for training, which feeds upon itself; a good training event leads to demand for more, and those who attend encourage others to come next time!

On a different level, working mainly with students, Navigators have increased their UK field staff from five in 1965 to twenty in 1975 and fifty in 1985, of whom ten are trainees. The emphasis of their basic work, as of the recently introduced 2:7 series on personal discipleship for group use in local churches,[25] is on deeper knowledge and application of the Bible and sharing that knowledge with others. As their members eventually settle into local churches they are a further trained resource for group leadership and personal work.

The same is true of Youth with a Mission. Their full-time staff and the whole scale of their operations has expanded tenfold in the last ten years. They now see 450-500 young people (average age twenty-two) each year on their main four to six month residential training courses, and over 2,000 in total on weekends or short summer schools. They estimate that 25% of their earlier students are now in full time Christian work, and 60% have some form of responsibility in their local church. British Youth for Christ and Operation Mobilisation, among others, have also seen dramatic growth in demand for training. The same interest is also reflected in the thousands of young people who each year flock to lectures, seminars and workshops on serious subjects at big events like Spring Harvest and Greenbelt—all of them new in the last ten years or so.

There is also explosive growth in demand for training in pastoral skills and counselling. For example, Crusade for World Revival, led by Selwyn Hughes, has run popular short residential courses in counselling for some years, for forty or so at a time. They are now starting more basic work on a much wider scale. Following an introductory ministers meeting, they held an initial one-day foundation course in Southampton last year, in a hall seating 500. This had to be repeated twice, to meet demand! Of the 1,350 who came to the first stage, 900 attended a second full day—at a slightly deeper level. Those who wish to go further, and whose churches are prepared to send them and then to use them, are now being offered a six-week course of evening classes. Meanwhile, a similar programme is under way in Preston, Lancs., and just starting in London.

Conclusion—hope for the church

The word training has deliberately been used in the widest possible sense, to include every type of activity which helps, in however small a way, to prepare and equip people to play a more responsible and effective part in the life of their local church. There is clearly a vastly greater amount of such activity about now than there was as little as five or ten years ago.

It may well be that some of it is of doubtful quality and that little has really yet reached into working-class areas; that there is duplication of effort, and lack of communication. It may also be true that some clergy simply don't know how to make the best use of trained lay people, and a few perhaps don't want to. It may be that some congregations are not yet prepared to face the change and the challenge which developing lay ministry requires.

In all these areas, there is need for patient persuasion, education, publicity, and for much more cross-fertilization of ideas. Possibly too much effort is being put into developing new training packages, and too little into monitoring the effectiveness of what is already available, and co-ordinating its development for wider use. It is certainly true that too many of those being trained receive little follow-up in putting into practice their initial enthusiasm; and that some have expected too much too soon, and have become disillusioned. Part of the reason for these shortcomings is simply that it is all so very new. Nonetheless, the number of lay people, perhaps particularly young people in their teens and twenties, who have been and are being involved in some form of training, has clearly risen very dramatically indeed over the last decade, and looks likely to go on rising as more resources become available and existing resources become more widely known. Where does all this lead us? What grounds for hope does it provide?

It may be helpful to offer a conclusion in the context of the Tiller Report *Strategy for Ministry*, which is currently under widespread discussion in the church. John Tiller underlines the need both for developing the ministry of every member, and for local leadership teams to make that possible. He also wants stipendiary ministry to be concentrated in more special- ist roles than that of the present 'General Practitioner' incumbent. This last point is the main focus of opposition to his proposals, because it has been taken to mean the gradual withdrawal of the full-time clergy from the parishes, when local leadership teams have become sufficiently established to manage on their own.

In practice, the experience of most growing churches which already have a substantial lay leadership team points in precisely the opposite direction. The more 'spare-time' leaders there are, the greater the need for the full-time theologically trained, professional; indeed in larger churches, for more than one. Even where there is a full-time 'lay' staff- administrator, lay pastor, community worker, or others, who may well be 'professional' in their own sphere, there is still a clearly felt need for the full-time leader, co-ordinator and theological resource for the whole team. In growing churches of all denominations, where there is a substantial 'eldership' team, spare-time or full-time or both together, the professional leader is in many ways like the second-century bishop surrounded by his team of presbyters and deacons. He is the overseer of the whole team. A key part of his task is to develop their gifts, and to be the person through whom the local church relates to neighbouring churches and organizations.

As churches grow, the number of full-time staff required in fact also grows. The explosion in lay-training, and the increasing experience of lay people in shared leadership, is producing a growing pool from which we can expect in due course to see emerging these increased numbers of full-time staff—both ordained and lay. Meanwhile, the immense variety and rapid development of training is at last beginning to equip people for the every member ministry to which the church has paid lip-service for so many years; and also for the sharing in leadership in the local churches which has begun to develop so recently.

Maybe none of the individual developments referred to above will, of themselves, make much visible difference on a national scale—although history reminds us of what can be achieved by even a small group trained and motivated under the Holy Spirit. But we are talking about thousands, indeed tens of thousands, as well as tens and hundreds, who have begun in the last ten years to receive training. This has never happened before. They are a new resource for every-member ministry; a new resource for shared leadership in the local church; a new recruiting ground for future full-time workers; all pointing to a time of growth in the church—in numbers, in maturity, and in its ability to obey Christ's command to go into all the world.

HOPE FOR THE CHURCH OF ENGLAND

by

Gavin Reid

There are two ways of looking at and talking about the Church of England.

We can look at it as a national institution. It has bishops, synods, ecclesiastical bureaucrats, cathedrals and historic buildings. It crowns monarchs, conducts royal weddings, makes statements, sets up commissions and so on. In this role of being the national ecclesiastical institution the Church of England is unique among the various denominations.

But there is another way of looking at and talking about the Church of England. It is a network of parish churches new and old in every corner of the land. It has thousands of parish priests, deaconesses and lay-workers, mostly in pastoral work. It has congregations of all shapes and sizes from a handful in some villages and inner cities to several hundred in some key suburban or city-centre churches.

When criticisms are made about 'the church losing its way' or 'meddling in politics' or 'throwing over its traditional beliefs' or 'being irrelevant to modern society', as often as not these judgements are directed against the national institution.

This is the case with much current criticism. There are many parish churches where numerical decline has been halted and even reversed. This is not the case in the majority of parishes, but it is true of enough situations to show that growth is a possibility in Anglican churches today. Decline is not inevitable.

Again, uncertainty about basic beliefs is not a problem in a good number of parish churches. There is no shortage of churches in the evangelical and catholic traditions where people say the Creed Sunday by Sunday without serious reservations. There is no lack of Anglican pulpits where the Ten Commandments are still presented as God's standard for human behaviour.

I know of many congregations where the ministry is shared between clergy and lay people in a creative way and where worship is imaginative and vibrant. The charismatic movement, while it has caused problems and divisions within some congregations, has brought a breath of fresh air into many.

Modern tunes, new songs and the use of guitar, electronic keyboards and even drums are not the evidence of a fawning trendiness—they are the signs of a genuine contemporary expression of Christian faith and worship.

One of the problems which the Church of England cannot avoid is that with parish churches covering every square inch of the country there are more possibilities of odd-ball clergy and unhappy relationships within congregations. In an age of mass media, what may in fact only be a local episode can be blown up into a story that is told nationwide. So the failings of individual clergy and congregations are told to the millions while the faithfulness of the majority never gets a mention.

If a vicar runs off with the wife of the churchwarden the nation will hear about it. If a deaconess visits a sick and despairing woman and coaxes her back into a healthy faith and confidence; or if someone preaches so effectively that several people in the congregation come to faith there and then—nobody is told, for such matters are not considered newsworthy.

So the general image of the Church of England is based on some of the things that happen at institutional level plus a series of stories of worst-case churches or clergy. Even many Christians in other denominations are misled into believing that this general image represents the truth.

Hope for the Church of England rests with the parish churches and I've seen enough of them to be optimistic. It is true that many of our parishes show little evidence of new life or growth but an ever-increasing number have exciting stories to tell and can see where they are going. Probably twenty per cent of our churches are growing numerically and I would guess that another thirty per cent have stopped shrinking. A Gallup poll in 1985 revealed that morale among the clergy was generally good especially among those working in the urban priority areas.

If things are healthy in the parishes then there is hope for the Church of England and I would maintain that the overall health of the parish churches is improving. Does this therefore mean that we can ignore the Church of England as a national institution? Can the Church operate and improve at ground level without bothering about its leadership and its historic structures?

The answer has to be 'no'. Things have changed considerably since the day when Karl Barth dismissed Anglican bishops as 'decorative general superintendents'. In today's diocese the bishop possesses real managerial power. If the proposals of the Tiller report are carried out the bishop would have even more. The majority of the clergy in a diocese would be under his immediate direction in an attempt to operate more flexibly than the present system allows.

The bishops we need must be skilled managers and pastoral strategists. Furthermore, they must be able to cope with the overobservation of local and national media.

In a strange way the episcopal nature of the Church of England is tailor-made for modern society. The press, radio and TV control the conversations and indeed the cohesion of a contemporary nation. To have a limited number of clearly identified leaders is to have exactly what the mass media need to focus and personalize information and opinion. Whether we like it or not, our bishops must be skilled at handling the media and they must be able to express orthodox Christian viewpoints succinctly and intelligibly to audiences (and reporters) who are theologically illiterate.

The leadership which affects the Church of England on the ground is part of that Church of England which, as the national institution, is conscious of the responsibilities that go with being the established church of the realm. It is here that part of our difficulty lies. The perceptions at this national level are often far removed from the realities that the vicar of an inner-city parish faces. The decisions affecting the training of clergy and the allocation of resources, for example, are made too far away from the firing line.

If there is to be hope for the Church of England the needs of the parish must dominate all appointments, procedures and decision-making. It may have been true that the Church could at one time think of itself as a secure and essential part of the nation's life, and that all it had to do was to maintain itself. The truth now is that in England the total attendance of the churches of all denominations stands at around ten per cent. Nine out of every ten people see little or no need to worship God. In such a situation the only proper vocation for a body calling itself the Church of England has to be a calling to evangelism. The controlling structures of the church must operate in such a way that the parishes are led and supported for mission.

This is not happening.

Let us consider the required qualities for a bishop. It seems to me that we choose men who are equipped to cope with the civic demands of the office and we have some excellent ecclesiastical diplomats and statesmen. In addition, those who make the choices seem to look for people who won't rock the boat by being too extreme in their theological position—and in a Church which contains competing traditions this is understandable. Definite evangelicals and definite Anglo Catholics make up a minority of the present bench of bishops and yet they represent the traditions which exhibit most commitment at local church level.

Let me say that I am trying to write this with no personalities in mind! I simply wish to make the point that if we want to see increasing effectiveness in our parishes then *the top leadership of the church must be dominated by men who have 'pounded the beat'* themselves and who, if circumstances required it, could move into a vicarage and do at least as good a job of things as any incumbent. We do not seem to count 'success' at parish level as a necessary ingredient in the qualifications of a diocesan bishop.

I cannot think of any progressive secular company that makes a practice of so ignoring operating success when it comes to promoting people to management status.

For the Church of England to have a future, therefore, it must move from a pastoral understanding of itself to a fundamentally evangelistic one. If we are the Church for an unevangelized nation our task is obvious.

A second essential, if the Church of England is to have an effective future, is that it must put its house in order doctrinally. In 1985 and 1986 the bishops have been working on a document *The nature of belief*. This was a direct response to the disquiet both inside and outside the ranks at the reported views of the Bishop of Durham, especially with regard to the virginal conception and the bodily resurrection of Jesus.

I am not convinced that a statement of this sort was the wisest response. The Church has plenty of doctrinal material set out on paper—the Creeds, the Thirty-Nine Articles and the doctrines enshrined in the Book of Common Prayer. When a priest or bishop is ordained according to the new forms of service he is questioned as to his acceptance of the 'holy Scriptures as revealing all things necessary for eternal salvation' and asked: 'Do you believe the doctrine of the Christian faith as the Church of England has received it, and in your ministry will you expound and teach it?'

It seems to me that we do not want more words about the content of our faith added to those we already have. What we want is for individual deacons, priests and bishops to take their ordination promises more seriously. And when this does not appear to be happening, then—as John Stott suggests in the first chapter—the Church has to exercise discipline more effectively.

For many people the issue is not whether they believe or disbelieve some credal statement. The problem, they would say, is: 'What does believing in such a doctrinal statement actually mean?' If, for example, we allow latitude in interpreting the meaning of the last things, should we not allow latitude in interpreting other areas of doctrine? Does a conviction about the resurrection of Christ necessitate holding to the view that the tomb was empty and that the body of Jesus revived?

The problem is a genuine one and this is not the place to attempt to grapple with it. A credal statement is, to some extent, an umbrella and can often give cover to more than one precise stance. However, the size and cover of the umbrella varies from one statement to another and there is less room for manoeuvre under some than under others! It would seem to me that the Church's firm commitment to Scripture makes it essential to say that Jesus was supernaturally conceived of a virgin, and that the resurrection of Jesus was of the body that died, leaving behind an empty tomb.

There are those who would argue that doctrinal firmness will not go hand in hand with a parish church seeking to serve and accept all within range. I do not agree. One can hold firm convictions and still deal with people lovingly 'where they are' and not necessarily where one would want them to be. If, however, we are calling people to follow Christ then it is surely obvious that we need to know what we mean by 'Christ' and that we have some clear ideas as to where he is going!

The third essential to the future of the Church of England is that the laity need to catch a vision of being members of the historic Christian community of the English people with a calling to witness to the nation at large. (Perhaps many of us in the ordained ministry need to recapture this vision also!)

One of the problems we face is widespread 'congregational pietism'. For a large number of worshippers the church is about a particular building and a particular group of people doing and saying things that are personally comforting. Any sense of mission—local, national or international—is alien and even threatening. Evangelism is what others do to others, or it is the activity of rather eccentric types of Christians. Making statements relating to social and public matters is 'meddling in politics'. Whole congregations can be united within such narrow understandings.

Somehow these blinkers have got to be removed and the tunnel vision of churchgoing as a resource to private religion needs to be replaced with a fuller more biblical set of perspectives. The Church is *God's* Church and it is 'of England'. We need to develop a sense of responsibility to the whole nation and to see this as part and parcel of worshipping God Sunday by Sunday in the local parish church.

Our failure to impart the grand vision of being the historic church committed to the English people has contributed to many of our keenest lay people leaving for other denominations and the new house churches. They have seen more vibrant worship elsewhere and felt that the parish church was 'holding them back'. While I believe the parish church should be able to find ways to meet the desires of those who want 'freer worship' and 'deeper biblical teaching' I also believe we need to help our more fervent members to recognize and rejoice in the responsibilities of being a church for the people of the parish as well as for the congregation.

I fully subscribe to the views and understandings expressed in Colin Buchanan's chapter. If one believes in being part of the one church in each place then the existence of choices of congregation in each place is a contradiction. We cannot rewrite history, and we have to recognize that many of the other denominations and independent churches began because of sins and failings within the Church of England. This leads me to my fourth essential for the church's future.

A commitment to the vision of a church that is truly 'of England' must carry with it an obligation to seek the united witness and action of all Christian bodies in any particular locality. This must not be from a paternalistic position but from a recognition that God's will is for the world to see Christians 'as one' within the community. The alternative is to pretend that other churches do not exist which is patently ridiculous.

If the Church of England is to have any future as the national church then, fifthly, it will have to come to terms with the fact that England is changing and becoming multi-cultural. We cannot lightly abandon various ethnic groups in the hope that they will be reached by the black churches or other more appropriate bodies. If we surrender one identifiable section of

English society we surrender also our title deeds.

We cannot expect a stereotyped parish system to be effective in every sort of area. The recent Archbishop's report on Urban Priority Areas rightly sees the need to rethink and rebuild the sort of Christian communities that are appropriate to such places. A costly effort is called for from the whole Church as the inner cities could be lost. Too easily the Church of England could become the Church of the Suburbs and Shires.

So is there hope for the Church of England? In the last resort the matter rests not with us or with our strategies. It rests with God himself.

It is remarkably easy to talk about the 'Church' and to leave God out of the discussion! Perhaps there are sections of this book which reveal such a tendency. The impressive and disturbing report *Faith in the City* managed to draw up sixty-one recommendations at the end of some 360 pages without needing to use the words 'God' or 'prayer' once.

If there is to be any hope for the Church of England it will need to be greatly blessed by God. It will need to learn more than it appears to have learned that the kingdom, the power and the glory belong to him and to him alone. It will need to believe in miracles, because the task of reclaiming England for Christ calls for mountains to be moved and the powers of darkness to be driven back.

It will need to see that the way towards discovering our destiny begins not in a committee room or synod debate but in the place where weeping people pray.

Notes

Chapter 6
1. *Rural Anglicanism*, p. 12. 2. *Rural Anglicanism*, p. 11. 3. *Rural Anglicanism*, p. 126. 4. *Rural Anglicanism*, p. 7.

Chapter 8
5. Andrew Walker, *Restoring the Kingdom* (Hodder & Stoughton, 1985).

Chapter 11
6. See Colin Buchanan's article 'Anglican Evangelicalism—the state of the "party"', *Anvil* Vol. 1, no. 1, pp. 7–18 for a good recent summary. 7. See Paul Marshall's book, *Thine is the Kingdom* (Marshalls, 1984) chapter 3, for a full exposition of this. 8. Peter Hinchliff, *Holiness and Politics* (Darton Longman & Todd, 1982), p. 194. 9. Graham Dow, *The Local Church's Political Responsibility* (Grove Pastoral Series No. 2, Nottingham, 1980). pp. 12–17. 10. Op. cit., p. 122. 11. Donald Reeves (ed.), *The Church and the State* (Hodder & Stoughton, 1984), chapter 4.

Chapter 12
12. *A New Pentecost*. 13. *Faith in the City* (The report of the Archbishop of Canterbury's Commission on Urban Priority Areas) (Church House Publishing, 1985), 6.67. The section 6.56f presents a most devastating critique of theological colleges to which the church must address itself. I personally believe that the colleges still have a most important role in forming the ministry of God's people although I am convinced that in the long run very radical changes will have to be made. Very probably within ten years there will be fewer residential colleges, but they will offer greater diversity of training than at the present time. One or two may offer advanced theological courses for 'higher fliers' but the rest will concentrate upon training for ministry, possibly incorporating some of the elements I mention in this chapter. I would personally welcome the demise of the independence of the theological colleges, and even a reduction in the number of colleges controlled by councils whose existence appears to be limited to ensuring the

perpetuation of rigid styles of church tradition. 14. *Faith in the City*, 6.60. 15. *Anglicans for Renewal* (Winter 1985, No. 19). 16. *Faith in the City*, 6.63.

Chapter 14

17. For example: Paul Minear, *Images of the Church in the New Testament* (1961); A. T. Hanson, *The Pioneer Ministry* (1961); R. Allen, *Missionary Methods, St Paul's or Ours* (1962); Mark Gibbs and T. Ralph Morton, *God's Frozen People* (1964); Michael Green, *Called to Serve* (1964); John Stott, *One People: Clergy and Laity in God's Church* (1969); ed. Clive Porthouse, *Ministry in the Seventies* (essays) (1970); Hans Kung, *Why Priests?* (1971); Ted Roberts, *Partners and Ministers* (1972); Karl Rayner, *The Shape of the Church to Come* (1972); Howard Snyder, *New Wineskins* (1975); Avery Dulles S. J., *Models of the Church* (1976); Michael Harper, *Let My People Grow* (1977); Edward Schillebeeckx, *Ministry a Case of Change* (1980); Paul Beasley Murray and Alan Wilkinson, *Turning the Tide* (1981); Michael Green, *Freed to Serve* (1983); Michael Saward, *All Change* (1983); Roy Pointer, *How do Churches Grow?* (1984). 18. From *Prospects for the Eighties—From a Census of the Churches in 1979: undertaken by the Nationwide Initiative in Evangelism* (Vol. 1: Bible Society, 1980; Vol. 2: MARC Europe, 1983). 19. *Shared leadership* is used as shorthand to cover a wide variety of degrees of sharing. At one extreme, almost total delegation, like the Bishop 'sharing his cure of souls' with the clergy; at the other, the idea (perhaps the dream) of complete equality. Neither of these seem desirable or practicable within a local church; there is seldom a case for total delegation, and there is little point in pretending to an equality which is clearly not real. Developments in the early church, and widespread evidence today, both indicate that in normal circumstances it is appropriate for there to be a clearly recognized 'leader of the leaders'—*primus inter pares*—who will obviously today be the full-time clergyman. This may be less obviously true when teams like this have been operating for 20 or 30 years. 20. In 1983, the writer visited 160 churches which were moving towards some form of shared leadership; a follow-up survey is now being undertaken. 21. According to the NIE Survey, this group was then less than 1% of the Protestant congregations in England. 22. 19 as Readers/Local Preachers; 8 as Stipendiary or Non-Stipendiary Ministers, including 4 deaconesses, and 3 in other full-time work. 23. The Chiltern Scheme was the model on which similar schemes have been set up in the other 2 counties of Oxford Diocese: all 3 work in a number of sub-centres, as well as centrally, and all Reader Training in the Diocese is now in their hands. Last year over 300 people took part in one or more of the Chiltern courses. 24. A team founded in 1982 and providing training for better leadership in local churches. 25. Title from Colossians 2:7: pilot scheme in 1983, now 50 groups of 8, in 25 churches, and expecting 30–40 new groups to start each year.

The Church of England
Where Is It Going?

by David Holloway

Your view of the Church of England will depend largely on your own experiences within its fine historical walls. You may know the warmth of Christian fellowship there, or you may think more of cold and decay.

Then there is the media's image. A slightly humorous, largely irrelevant organization, where ornate buildings and unknown bishops conspire to keep Christianity away from the twentieth century in a breathtaking blur of indecision and doctrinal haze.

So when the spotlight fell on the personal views of the Bishop of Durham, the whole Church seemed to be on trial: what *does* it believe about the Virgin Birth of Jesus, and his Empty Tomb?

David Holloway is one of the clergy in the North-East most anxious to clear the mist of uncertainty and debate. Here he provides an in-depth assessment of the doctrinal and practical issues raised by the controversy. The result is a strategy for both clergy and people, to take up their responsibility to God and the nation—before it is too late.

David Holloway is Vicar of Jesmond, Newcastle-upon-Tyne.

K *Kingsway Publications*

The Great Evangelical Disaster

by Francis A. Schaeffer

Are Christians still a voice to the society in which they live? Do they speak out for truth and morality with a clear, uncompromising call, charged with the authority that should be the hallmark of the people of God?

Francis Schaeffer gives his answer in the pages of this, his last book. With a prophetic zeal that is tempered by a deep love for Christ's people, Dr Schaeffer exposes the insidious growth of compromise that has wormed its way into the evangelical church. The result is an urgent challenge to Christians everywhere to re-examine the basics of their Christian life and commitment, and so turn the tide of secular humanism that threatens to engulf our whole culture.

DR FRANCIS A. SCHAEFFER (1912–1984) is widely recognized as one of the most influential thinkers in the church this century. He is the author of 23 books, which have been translated into 25 languages. With his wife Edith he founded L'Abri Fellowship, an international Christian community with branches in Switzerland, England, Holland, Sweden, France, and the USA.

k
Kingsway Publications

Build That Bridge

by David Coffey

The last twenty years have witnessed some significant moves towards visible Christian unity. It is no longer possible to label a Christian by his church name and then confidently suppose that you know his every belief and attitude. The church—the whole church—is in ferment, and barriers are being shaken.

Yet there is still division.

David Coffey seeks to bring the guidance of a pastor's heart into two aspects of that division:

— first, he asks Christians within the same local church to face renewal and change without needless division or carnal schism:

— secondly, he asks church leaders to be prepared to talk to each other across the varying divides in a spirit of mutual recognition.

This is a book that asks searching questions, but never leaves us without a hope of an answer.

'I heartily commend this admirable and timely book. It is, in my view, well written, warm, almost passionate in tone, always interesting, very fair and genuinely open'.

PHILIP GREENSLADE
The King's Church, Aldershot

'May this be a launching pad to send folk exploring regions beyond where even this far-sighted author hoped to send them'.

COLIN BUCHANAN
Bishop of Aston

DAVID COFFEY is Senior Pastor of Upton Vale Baptist Church in Torquay, and President of the Baptist Union 1986–87. He is married with two children.

Large format paperback

Kingsway Publications